Smith Wigglesworth

Harrison House

Shippensburg, PA

Smith Wigglesworth

Powerful Messages for
Living a Radical Life

compiled by

ROBERTS LIARDON

The sermons in this book are from the Smith Wigglesworth Collection in the Assemblies of God Archives, Springfield, Missouri, and are used with permission.

Published by Harrison House Publishers Shippensburg, PA 17257

ISBN 13 TP: 978-1-6803-1572-1

ISBN 13 eBook: 978-1-6803-1573-8

ISBN 13 HC: 978-1-6803-1575-2

ISBN 13 LP: 978-1-6803-1574-5

Previously published under 978-1-6068-3426-8

For Worldwide Distribution, Printed in the U.S.A.

1 2 3 4 5 6 7 8 / 25 24 23 22 21

Contents

Chapter 1

Smith Wigglesworth

(1859–1947)

by Roberts Liardon

O nly believe!"

"I'm a thousand times bigger on the inside than on the outside!"

"Fear looks; faith jumps!"

These statements were heard by thousands of people who sat under one of the most unique ministries of this century: *the ministry of Smith Wigglesworth.* His ministry has survived successfully for more than forty years since his death in 1947. It is of importance to state that for a ministry to be producing eternal results this far after its natural conclusion means that the head of the ministry lived a life of obedience and spoke words of life more than opinion and views.

I have spent many exciting hours reading Smith Wigglesworth's sermons and interviewing people who knew him or attended his Gospel crusades. Many describe him with the same adjectives, such as "authoritative, bold, compassionate, very challenging," calling him a "man of eternal value" who lived a "life full of faith."

I have collected sermons that Smith Wigglesworth preached under "divine unction." Some of them are lengthy and others are short. I believe that these sermons will lift you to new horizons in your personal relationship with Jesus. The cry of the Spirit that came through Wigglesworth can still be heard today through these sermons.

Wigglesworth—The Early Years

Smith Wigglesworth was born in Menston, Yorkshire, England, on June 10, 1859. Throughout his childhood, Wigglesworth was extremely poor and received no education. He could not write but only sign his name, even as an adult.

At the tender age of six, he began working full time on a farm. When he was seven years old, he started working with his father in the mills, six days a week, twelve to fourteen hours each day.

When he was eight, he was converted at a Wesleyan Methodist meeting, which he attended with his grandmother. He soon became a soul winner and led his own mother to faith in Christ. Five years later, on September 5, 1872, Wigglesworth was confirmed by a bishop. He experienced a strong presence of God for several days after that.

Also at the age of thirteen, he moved with his parents from his hometown of Bradford. When he was sixteen, he began to work for the Salvation Army there, giving his Sundays to prayer and fasting.

Then Wigglesworth began plumbing. He recalled, "When I was eighteen years of age, I went to a plumber to ask for employment. I cleaned up my shoes with an extra shine, put on a clean collar, and applied at the home of the man who was the owner of Bradford's finest plumbing business. He said, "No, I don't need anyone."

"The man let me walk down to his gate and then called me back, saying, 'There's something about you that is different. I just can't let you go!'"

Polly the Preacher

In 1877, Wigglesworth, now a young man, attended a meeting and saw a girl called "Polly" converted. He knew she would become his wife.

His life from that point began to grow concerning the work of the Lord. By the time he was twenty years old, he was believing God for about fifty souls to be born again every week. He moved to Liverpool and began to minister to young people there, using his faith all the while.

In 1882, Wigglesworth moved back to Bradford and married Mary Jane (Polly) Featherstone, who had been raised in a Methodist family. She was outgoing, intelligent, and beautiful. Before long, he began to try to preach because Polly was a preacher and wanted him to be one, too. But he couldn't talk very well. He gave preaching a few tries, but he would get embarrassed and discouraged and leave the stage. One day he finally told his wife, "I'll never do that again!"

Smith Wigglesworth didn't become a preacher at that point, but he did become a father before long. He and Polly had five children from their union: a daughter, Alice, and sons Seth, Harold, Ernest, and George.

Unfortunately, Wigglesworth spent two years in a spiritual "wilderness" in his life. He lacked commitment to God. His business, however, was doing very well at that time.

Praise God, at age twenty-six, Wigglesworth returned to God with a new zeal. He began to work in what we call "the children's ministry." He would get a pony, go to the streets, put little children on it, and take them to church. He would teach them about the Lord, then he would take them back home. That's the way he worked for the Lord.

Hungry for the Word

Wigglesworth was a man with a hunger for God's Word. His hunger pains were almost constant, with little relief for him, however, because he could not read. To satisfy his great hunger for God's Word, he learned to read by a supernatural act of the Lord and with help from his wife.

How he loved God's Word! It's said that he never went fifteen minutes without reading the Bible.

That same year, Wigglesworth spent ten days "waiting" upon the Lord. It was worth it. He received what he described as "new life" from Him.

"Jesus Will Heal You!"

The healing ministry came into England in the late 1880s. Wigglesworth had never come across anything like it. One day he went to a mission in a nearby city, where they were praying for the sick. For the very first time, he saw people being healed, people being made whole, by the power of Jesus. He was so excited! He went out into the streets, found sick people, and said, "Come with me. I know a place where you can be made whole. I know a place where you can be prayed for and Jesus will heal you!"

He took them back into the mission and saw many of those people born again and healed.

Then he himself began to pray for the sick. He ministered his first healing when he was asked to substitute for the leaders of some meetings in Keswick. Praying for the sick became a part of his life and ministry. He went on to establish the Bowland Street Mission, through which he brought healing to Bradford. Wigglesworth became very successful in both the mission and his business.

Healing in Jesus' Name

Smith Wigglesworth experienced the power of God in many wonderous ways. In the early 1900s, he was healed of hemorrhoids, which he had had since childhood, when a fellow minister prayed in agreement with him. He received another healing while deathly ill. He stated to his wife, "It seems to me that this is my home call. To protect yourself, you should now call a physician."

The doctor came and, upon examining him, reported that Wigglesworth had been made weak by appendicitis, which he apparently had had for more than six months. He was doubtful of Wigglesworth's strength to undergo surgery.

After the doctor's departure, an elderly woman, accompanied by a young man, arrived armed for prayer. The young man laid his hands on Wigglesworth. He cried, "Come out, devil, in the Name of Jesus!"

Immediately, Wigglesworth received his strength back. "To my surprise, I felt as well as I had ever been in my life," he recalled.

So Wigglesworth got up and went to work. When the doctor came back that same afternoon and discovered that Wigglesworth had gone to work, he commented, "They'll bring him back a corpse, as sure as you live."

After that time, the Wigglesworth's pledged, "From henceforth, no medicine, no doctors, no drugs of any kind shall come into our house"; however, they never imposed their decision on others.

Wigglesworth did his best to present God's healing/saving power to those who needed it. On February 13, 1904, the vilest man in Bradford was saved when Wigglesworth provided a banquet of fine foods for many sick, poor, and oppressed people.

An hour and a half of "entertainment" following the meal, consisted of people giving testimonies of physical healings they had received at the mission. Wigglesworth then ended the time together in his unconventional way, calling out, *"Who wants to be healed?"*

Wigglesworth was an unpredictable man, but sometimes God seemed to be just as unpredictable toward him. The morning of October 26, 1907, he was knocked to the floor, not once but three times, by the power of God during prayer.

The Baptism in the Spirit Brings Power!

Far beyond these displays of God's power in his life, the greatest thing that happened to him, aside from his salvation experience, was the baptism in the Holy Spirit. On October 28, 1907, at age forty-eight, Smith Wigglesworth received the baptism of the Holy Spirit in an Anglican church pastored by Alexander Boddy.

Remember, Wigglesworth was a man who could not talk well. His tongue was tied. He stuttered and stammered. His wife was the one who did the preaching. But when he received the baptism of the Holy Spirit, his tongue was loosed and he could speak. He instantly became a great preacher!

Upon receiving the baptism of the Holy Spirit, he went back to a meeting where his wife was preaching. He said, "I want to preach tonight. I want to do these things."

Naturally, it amazed Polly. It *shocked* her. She didn't know what to do but say, "'All right, we'll let you preach. We'll let you do these things."

Wigglesworth took the pulpit, and the first few moments, I understand through his writings, he stuttered as usual. But then the anointing of God came upon him. Something began to happen. He began to teach and preach *clearly*. There was no disturbance in his language. His speech was no longer impaired. The words flowed like a river. He gave all the credit for what was happening to the baptism in the Holy Spirit.

That night, fifty people were baptized with the Holy Spirit and spoke in tongues after his first anointed sermon!

Five years later, Wigglesworth was still seeing wonderful results while preaching at that church. The May 31, 1912 issue of the Sunderland *Daily Echo* reported the results of Wigglesworth's meetings there. It gave detailed accounts of several healings and the deliverance of two people who were demon possessed. (One was a demon-possessed man Wigglesworth had intercepted on the man's way to drown himself in the sea.)

It became obvious that Wigglesworth was well acquainted with the healing ministry. People tried to draw from his wisdom on the subject. When asked one time to recommend a good book on divine healing, he simply stated that he know of only one: the Word of God. He believed that one sentence was like a sermon, able to change one's course entirely.

Boldness and Authority in Ministry

The ministry of healing under Smith Wigglesworth was very different from what we are used to seeing today. He was a bold man. He was a strong man, like a statesman is. He didn't always pray for the sick with a "nice" laying on of hands. I'm sure he did that sometimes, but he was mainly known for his gruffness in dealing with people. He would lay hands on them boldly and authoritatively, being very rough at times.

Most preachers do things casually. They "suggest" things for people and the devil to do, which brings minimum results. We need to be like Smith Wigglesworth; *we need to be bold and authoritative* (but never rude). Now, being like this may bring persecution from those around us, but it also will bring the results people need. It will bring healing!

Smith Wigglesworth's ministry was similar to a bull in a china shop. Many times if people came in his prayer line more than once after they'd already been prayed for, he would tell them, "I prayed for you once—go sit down! That's enough!"

Some folks were upset with him at this. A lot of people around him, including a lot of other ministers, said, "Brother Wigglesworth, calm down. Quit being so rough. Quit being so mean."

They didn't know what to do with him, yet they couldn't deny that he was having better results than they were. They couldn't outdo the miracles that were in his ministry.

You never have a right to criticize someone until you have outdone the miracles that have been done in his ministry. Even then, you'll lovingly be voicing "constructive criticism."

Dead or Healed?

Dr. Lester Sumrall of South Bend, Indiana, is a man who used to visit Smith Wigglesworth and who preached with him many times.

His personal accounts of the way Wigglesworth ministered to the sick are very interesting. This is one of the stories he tells:

"In the same church where I was preaching, the great Glad Tidings Tabernacle, which seated more than three thousand people at that time, Wigglesworth was preaching in a Sunday afternoon healing service. They brought people from hospitals, in wheelchairs, portable hospital beds, etc., for Smith Wigglesworth to pray for them. From one of the local hospitals, a doctor brought a very severe cancer case. Actually, he hadn't wanted to bring him, because the man was so near death.

"I went over and sat beside his little hospital bed on the platform. Here came Smith Wigglesworth, who was a bit gruff, down the line, praying for the people.

"The way he would ask you what was wrong with you was this: 'What's up?'

"In his part of England, that was a familiar way of speaking. *'What's up?'* was the same as saying, 'What ails you? What is wrong with you?'

"He got to this cancer patient who was stretched out on the bed, wearing a little hospital gown that had no buttons up the back. The doctor was sitting there with his stethoscope in his ears, listening to the man's heartbeat and letting everyone know the man was very near death. When Wigglesworth said, 'What's up?' the doctor replied, 'He is dying of cancer.'

"Wigglesworth said, 'Where is it?'

"The doctor said, 'In his stomach.'

"And Smith Wigglesworth, probably the most unusual person I have ever met in my life, wound up his arm and with his fist hit him where the cancer was, right in the stomach! The man's hands fell off the bed, and the doctor screamed, 'He's dead! He's dead!'

"Then the doctor looked up and said, 'You killed him! You killed him! The family will sue you. You killed him!'

"Smith Wigglesworth wasn't upset one bit. He said, 'Ee's healed.' (That's the way he'd say, 'He's healed'; he didn't pronounce h's.) He said, 'He's healed'; and he didn't stop. He just went on down the line, praying.

"About ten minutes later, here came the man! He'd gotten up off the hospital bed, moved the doctor to one side, and begun to walk in that funny little hospital gown that was open in the back. Here he was, following Smith Wigglesworth, with his hands up in the air, praising God! He said, 'I have no pain. I feel wonderful inside. I have energy I have not had for I don't know how long.'

"Smith Wigglesworth was so unusual. He didn't turn around and say, 'Oh, thank God! Praise God! Everybody, look at it!'

"This sort of thing was so normal with him, he said, 'Well, just thank God for it; and he went on praying for people.'"

"Moved by What I Believe"

Why didn't the sight of that man who lay motionless after Wigglesworth's punch shake Wigglesworth up and make him think that he had failed—or worse, that GOD had failed? Wigglesworth once said, "I am not moved by what I see. I am only moved by what I believe."

And he believed the man was healed!

Smith Wigglesworth was a very unusual man, like Dr. Sumrall said. He had the philosophy, which he stated many times, that "Anybody can be ordinary, but it takes someone with faith in God to be *extra*ordinary."

I believe his life and ministry were just that: extraordinary.

Polly Is Raised From the Dead

I want to tell you another story that will challenge your faith to be as strong in the Lord as Wigglesworth's was. What that man had we can have, too, if we'll pay the price for it, if we'll get into the Word and prayer, build our faith, and make our inner man strong. God can give us the ability to be extraordinary.

Every life and every ministry is to be unique. But they're all to be lives and ministries built on faith in God, like Wigglesworth's.

Smith Wigglesworth's wife died on January 1, 1913. He was preaching a meeting when the news came to him. He finished the meeting and then went to her. Of course, she was dead when he got there—so he raised her from the dead and began to talk to her. He said, "Why are you going?" and asked her questions along these lines.

God finally said to him, *"She's mine. She's through with the work. Let her go."*

He laid his wife down, and she went back to heaven.

It's true—God CAN bring a person to life again. By God's power, Smith Wigglesworth raised at least fourteen people from the dead. Some say there were more.

Strength in the Inner Man

Smith Wigglesworth was a man who had the rare ability to inoculate you with faith when he preached. He lived out of the strength of his inner man, and he could inject this strength, this believing power, into people's hearts.

The word spread about this anointed, turn-of-the century preacher who followed Jesus and about the works he did.

On May 16, 1913, the front page of England's *Daily Mirror* newspaper featured four photographs of Smith Wigglesworth. Accompanying the photographs were these headlines: "Five Pentecostals Baptized in the Sea—Woman Falls Prostrate after Immersion in Icy Water." It was extremely unusual for the British press to place religious news on the front page of its most widely read national daily newspaper. But they did, glory to God!

Miracles, Revival, Glory!

Now I'm going to give you an almost yearly account of Smith Wigglesworth's life. I will briefly cover the remaining years. The information is sketchy at times, but it is vital to help us understand what made this man the great man of faith that he was, as evidenced in his dynamic ministry.

In 1914, Smith Wigglesworth began his international ministry in Canada and the United States. He preached there many times throughout the following thirty years. As a result, a large number of salvations and healings occurred.

Each spring, Smith held a convention in Bradford which was open to all. In the spring of 1914, it was reported that he collected about $6,000 from the people for missions. The next year he got $6,750.

Although these figures went up, Wigglesworth had cause for deep sorrow as well as rejoicing that year. A tragedy happened in his family. His youngest son, George, died.

Our account of his life picks up five years later when he traveled to France, Switzerland, and Sweden. In Sweden, he experienced persecution from medical doctors and religious leaders. Swedish officials prohibited Wigglesworth from laying hands on people. He prayed for them as a group while each person laid hands on himself. Hundreds of healings resulted. He called them "wholesale healings."

In Stockholm, he preached to twenty thousand people in an open-air meeting held with the leading Swedish Pentecostal, Lewis Pethrus. In another city where Wigglesworth spoke, a man who had been deaf for forty years was healed.

His healing ministry didn't stop or slow down as Wigglesworth grew older. At the end of 1921, he preached in Ceylon (now called "Sri Lanka") and India. The greatest results were those in Columbo (Sri Lanka). Wigglesworth preached by way of interpreters in 120-degree temperatures and prayed for about five hundred sick people each night. At the beginning of these meetings, he passed through the thousands of people who could not get inside for lack of room. As they reached out and touched him, they were healed!

It's recorded that, from February to March of 1922, he preached in Australia and a six-year-old girl who had never walked was healed. A man who had been deaf for twenty years also was healed, along with his wife, who had been in a wheelchair for more than six years.

Two months later, Wigglesworth brought "Pentecost" to New Zealand. Although he spent only a few months there, it was reported that thousands were saved, healed, and filled with the Holy Spirit. Many felt it was the greatest spiritual revival they had had for more than a century. Today, several Pentecostal organizations exist in New Zealand because of the meetings he held there.

Wigglesworth returned to New Zealand and Australia the next year. He also preached at Central Bible College in Springfield, Missouri.

In 1924, *Ever Increasing Faith*, a book of his sermons, was published. Royalties were donated to Zaire missions.

In 1925, he preached for Maria Woodworth-Etter at her home church, the Etter Tabernacle. He toured Europe and was arrested in Switzerland twice for supposedly practicing medicine without a license.

In all of his travels, he was impressed the most at Angelus Temple in Los Angeles, California. Angelus Temple was pastored by Aimee Semple McPherson. He felt the unction to preach greater there than in any other place in the world.

At age seventy-two, Smith Wigglesworth asked God for fifteen more years to be added to his lifespan. After suffering six years with gallstones, deliverance came. It was gladly welcomed, for he had agonized greatly during that time. "Trying to pass the stones, he often rolled on the floor in agony," his daughter reported. "Night after night, he was in and out of his bed."

In 1936, he ministered in Africa with the Apostolic Faith Mission, founded by John G. Lake. He received a vision of a great outpouring of the Spirit on "mainline" denominations and delivered a prophecy to David du Plessis, who was to play a big part in the fulfillment of that vision. Du Plessis was so instrumental in that outpouring that people nicknamed him "Mr. Pentecost."

On March 5, 1947, Wigglesworth was sitting in his home with a friend. He commented to his guest, "Today in my mail I had an invitation to Australia, one to India and Ceylon (Sri Lanka), and one to America. People have their eyes on me.

"Oh, Wigglesworth," he wept. "What a failure to think that people have their eyes on me. God will never give His glory to another; He will take me from the scene."

Seven days later, on March 12, 1947, Smith Wigglesworth died. He was nearly eighty-eight when he went home to be with the Lord.

Despite his advanced age, Wigglesworth didn't die sick; he died very, very healthy. He was at a funeral, which is an odd place for someone to die, and asked a man how a certain person he had prayed for was doing. When the man turned around to answer him, Wigglesworth just fell into his arms .

You don't have to die sick. You don't have to die out of the ministry, having been forced out of it by sickness. You can be in the ministry until you leave this earth. And you are *supposed* to leave it in a *blaze* of glory! Leave full of the health and strength God Almighty supplies His people.

Usually when someone dies, everyone automatically says, "Well, I wonder what sickness this person died of?"

Too many people have died the wrong way. God's way is for us to die in the fiery, brilliant light of His glory. Proverbs 4:18 says that the day of the righteous is supposed to grow *brighter* and *brighter*, not dimmer and dimmer. It's time we began to realize the truth in that and expect it to happen in our lives!

The older generation does not need to fade away. Their days can be bright. They can be strong all the days of their lives, right along with the next generation. The next generation should be strong, too.

The older generation is the rudder for the great Gospel ship. They keep it on the right course. We need the kind of ministry the older generation offers, for they will challenge and wisely direct the young. The young will make mistakes, but if older believers are there to help them, they won't fall because of those mistakes.

Bigger Inside Than Outside

We've studied a lot about what Smith Wigglesworth did. Now let's see what he said, for his words reflect the faith that was in his heart.

Jesus said:

Out of the abundance of the heart the mouth speaketh.

Matthew 12:34

The apostle Paul linked words and faith together, saying that the spirit of faith is:

I believed, and therefore have I spoken.

2 Corinthians 4:13

Smith Wigglesworth often said, "I'm a thousand times bigger on the inside than I am on the outside."

He was a thousand times bigger on the inside than on the outside because he built up his inner man. One of the greatest secrets you can get from studying about Smith Wigglesworth is this: *Your inner man needs to be as strong, if not stronger than, the gift and anointing God has given you to carry on His ministry in the earth.*

Many people only have an anointing for the pulpit and have none for their own lives. To live daily in God's anointing, you must be a thousand times bigger on the inside than you are on the outside. You must build up your inner man, like Wigglesworth did. Build it up by reading the Word and by praying with tremendous intensity, or fervency.

> *The effectual fervent prayer of a righteous man availeth much.*
>
> James 5:16

Paul told Timothy to *"stir up the gift of God"* that was within him (2 Timothy 1:6). Live in the "stirring ups" of God, so your faith will always be active and moving.

Full of the Spirit and Hungry for More

Smith Wigglesworth said, "I'd rather have on my platform a group of people who are full of the Holy Spirit and are hungry than to have a group of ministers who are satisfied with their relationship with the Lord."

I'm the same way. I'd rather have a few young people who are starving for God or for more of God than a group of people who had a great move of God and saw a great anointing at one time but today are satisfied with their position. The position they are in is called "backsliding."

You can do good works and still be a backslider. In fact, you can be a preacher who regularly preaches Gospel sermons and be backslid. Backsliding has to do with your lack of *hunger* for God.

If you aren't hungry for God, you will slide backwards in your walk with Him.

Your hunger for God is to be continuous! It's supposed to make you go higher and higher, to new realms of the Spirit. Never be shallow. Always go for a greater glory—from one height of faith to the next height of faith. That's the way Smith Wigglesworth lived, and that's the way you and I need to live in order to obey God and do what we are called to do.

Break Through the Barriers

Smith Wigglesworth said, "I'd rather die trusting God than live a whole life of unbelief."

His entire life revolved around trust in God. It's time for us to get to where trust in God is our life. We need to have faith in Him and reject all unbelief.

Many of the people around Smith Wigglesworth were scared of him, because he never came out of his God-given position in the kingdom of God. He had faith, and he never quit believing God. He had boldness, and he never quit being bold. He had strength, and he never quit being strong in the Lord. He was called, and He never quit being the powerful minister God wanted him to be.

One reason people may not respect the gift and the call of God in you is because you don't live in it night and day. If you live in the faith, boldness, strength, and power of God every day— whether you are eating breakfast, relaxing, or just having normal conversation with someone—they'll respect you. They'll honor you. They'll come to you and want to be prayed for by you.

Of course, these people may get a little nervous around you. A lot of people were nervous around Smith Wigglesworth, but that didn't hinder him. He'd just keep going. If a meeting was tough, he'd take off his jacket and "bust it through" in the Spirit. He'd charge forward with his faith and break right through the enemy's barriers, setting the captives free!

We've got to learn to "bust through" again. If there was ever a day when preachers needed to learn to break the devil's barriers for spiritual victories, it's today. Like Wigglesworth did, ministers need to break the barriers and tear down the walls so that people can walk through to the promised land of victory!

A Man of Compassion

The last time Dr. Sumrall saw him, Smith Wigglesworth blessed him. Although Smith Wigglesworth was very bold and authoritative, he also was compassionate, as we see in this story Dr. Sumrall tells:

"I was living in England when the war broke out in 1939. Hitler's armies were in Belgium, Holland, and France. The British government sent a special agent to my room at a Bible school in London to tell me, 'We will be next. This is now a war zone. You are a visitor here, so you'll have to leave the country.'

"I went to tell some friends the news. One of them was Smith Wigglesworth. By now, we were old friends. I was twenty-five or twenty-six, and he was eighty. We were like an Abraham and an Isaac, or a Paul and a Timothy.

"I went to his home and broke the news to him. Then I said, 'Brother Wigglesworth, the fellowship with you has been very rare. I have been greatly blessed by you. I humbly thank the Lord and thank you for giving me so much of your time. Thank you for letting me hear you talk to God in your prayers and read the living Word of God and see how it comes alive within you. I am so grateful. And now I must leave.'

"He stood up on his feet. He looked like a Philadelphia lawyer or a Boston banker. His hair was never out of place. He was always groomed so perfectly and beautifully. He stood there like a general and said, 'I want to bless you.'

"He had done that a lot of times. But this time, he laid his hand over on me and pulled me close to him. I let my head go in close to him. Tears flowed down his face and dropped off onto my forehead and ran down my face. He cried, 'God, O God, let all of the faith that is within my heart be within his heart. Let the knowledge of God that resides in me also reside in him. Let all the gifts of the Spirit that function in my ministry function in his life.'

"I just stood there weeping; he stood there praying and weeping, holding me in an embrace to him. I felt the holy anointing of the Most High God as it flowed from him into me."

Fear Looks; Faith Jumps

Smith Wigglesworth believed that there are two essential ingredients for a successful ministry: (1) the Holy Spirit must operate in your life and in your meetings, and (2) you must have personal holiness. These are requirements for having all that God wants in every meeting.

Wigglesworth also said, "When it comes down to faith, it can be summed up in the words: Only believe." What a simple theology!

You could contain Smith Wigglesworth's whole message in that one phrase: *Only believe.* No wonder his favorite chapter in the Bible was Hebrews 11, "The Faith Chapter."

Speaking on the subject of faith, he also would say, "Fear looks, but faith jumps."

Our faith in God is supposed to leap forward. It's got to jump out at the devil and send him running!

One time Wigglesworth was waiting for a bus to come. He was observing a lady and a dog following her. The lady kept playing with the dog and talking to it. All of a sudden, she saw the bus coming. She told the dog, "Now, go home. Go on home."

The dog didn't understand her. As the bus kept corning closer and closer, she finally screamed, "Go home!" and the dog took off.

Brother Wigglesworth thought to himself, *You know, that's what we have to do to the devil. We have to speak loud enough and be bold enough so that he, and everyone around him, understands that we've said, "Go home and leave me alone!"*

This generation of Christians is going to have to get bold against the devil. Authority and strength have to come in so the devil will get out!

Be Strong in Faith!

Pertaining to the healing ministry of the future, Smith Wigglesworth said, "I can see a day when the ministry of healing is going to get more difficult. There are already too many remedies in which people put their trust. But I can see that it will get worse, until it will be hard to get people to believe at all."

When his ministry began, medical science was not as we know it today. Still, no matter how great medical science has become, *Jesus Christ* is the One who can heal you and make you whole. Even if you are terminally ill, God can heal you! He healed people in Wigglesworth's day, and He will heal you today! His power never faints. It's always the same—and STRONGER, if you will only believe it's so.

Thank God for a man like Smith Wigglesworth, who pioneered the Pentecostal Movement and healing through Jesus' Name throughout the nations of the world. Everywhere he went, great revivals broke out and great miracles happened. And his powerful ministry is still having an effect upon *this* generation.

Will your ministry have the same kind of effect when you die? Will it be as effective even while you live? To have a ministry that produces eternal results, learn from Wigglesworth to have faith in God. Receive strength from God. Believe God for His power. Break down all barriers of the devil. Be bold and be loud!

Yes, be LOUD! The devil doesn't like people to be loud. But God does; sometimes loudness is very much a part of what He wants to do. Remember, Jesus raised Lazarus from the dead by standing outside the tomb and yelling, *"Lazarus, come forth"* (John 11:43).

There is a degree of loudness that belongs in the Church today. It belongs in the pulpit, it belongs in the pew, and it belongs in the home. The devil sometimes acts like he's deaf. If you raise your voice of authority at him, he'll hear you and leave you alone.

Wigglesworth gave people who want to be effective ministers for God another piece of advice. He said, "Never look back if you want the power of God in your life."

It's true—those who look back will never have the power of God in their lives. If you look back, that's where you are going to be: back in the past. Never look back; always go forward. It's the present and the future that keep you alive, that keep you on the cutting edge. And when you are living on the cutting edge, it's the strength of God that keeps you up there.

The Luxury of Being Spirit-filled

We know how important the baptism in the Holy Spirit was to Smith Wigglesworth. He said, "It is a luxury to be filled with the Spirit."

Many people take the infilling of the Spirit for granted. They say "Well, I'm filled with the Spirit and everything's fine."

But when you look closely at what it is to be filled with the Spirit and have the ability to speak in other tongues as God gives the utterance, you appreciate it more. You see that it is a great luxury to have the Third Person of the Godhead inside you.

Oh, what a blessing it is! "If you want to be filled with the Spirit, you'll have a constant spring in your life," Wigglesworth said, adding, "and your faith will always be centered around the Lord Jesus Christ."

The infilling of the Holy Spirit will cause you to lift up Jesus. JESUS is to be glorified in our lives!

Wigglesworth also stated, "It is impossible to overestimate the importance of being filled with the Spirit."

It is impossible for us to meet the conditions of the present day, and to walk in the light as He is in the light, without the baptism in the Holy Spirit. One reason Smith Wigglesworth was so strong and had such great miracles in his life and ministry was because of the baptism in the Holy Spirit. He told people, "Never say, 'I can't,' if you are filled with the Holy Spirit."

Oh, how he depended on the Holy Spirit! This is the main thing that stands out to me about Smith Wigglesworth: He knew how to stand in the power of the Holy Spirit. His faith never wavered, but always centered on Jesus, as the Spirit wanted it to be. His sermons focused on what I call "The Forgotten Man of Today": Jesus Christ. Too few sermons center around Jesus anymore. But if you preach and will center your life and messages of faith and hope in the Man, the Son of God, Jesus Christ, wonders will be done through you! Oh, the power that God will use through you!

Wigglesworth's life was challenging. His was not a normal life. But then, the Christian life is not to be normal. Life in Christ is not a natural life; it's a *supernatural* life.

What this man, Smith Wigglesworth, had is not past. His life on the earth is past; but, as we saw earlier, the strength of God, the call of God, and the anointing of God are still the same for us today. We continue to hear from God through Wigglesworth's sermons and be changed by the power of the Word and the testimonies of what the Spirit did in his ministry.

The blessings and revelation received by those who first heard Wigglesworth can be ours today, for his message came from One who is greater than he. It has an eternal touch of divinity within. It is not man-made—it is *the cry of the Spirit!*

Chapter 2

Cry of the Spirit

by Smith Wigglesworth

I am the voice of one crying in the wilderness, Make straight the way of the lord, as said the prophet Esaias.

John 1:23

...Repent ye: for the kingdom of heaven is at hand...
Then went out to him Jerusalem, and all Judaea, and all the region round about Jordan,
And were baptized of him in Jordon, confessing their sins.

Matthew 3:2, 5, 6

John the Baptist's raiment was camel's hair; his girdle, leather; his meat, locusts and wild honey. John was without the food and clothing that he was used to at the priestly home of his earthly father.

He had only a groan, a cry: *the cry of the Spirit.*

No angels, shepherds, wise men, or stars heralded his immediate coming. (But the heavenly messenger Gabriel, who spoke to Daniel and to Mary, spoke also to his father, Zacharias, about his birth and call.) Yet from his obscure place in the wilderness, he moved the whole land. God through him cried the cry of the Spirit—oh, that awful, piercing cry!—and all the land was moved by it.

Some are ashamed to cry. Others don't want to because there is a loneliness in a cry. But they really aren't alone—GOD is with a person who has only a cry.

A New Thing

God spoke to John in the wilderness and told him of a new thing: water baptism.

> *And John bare record, saying, I saw the Spirit descending from heaven...and it abode upon him.*
>
> *And I knew him not: but he that sent me to baptize with water, the same said unto me, Upon whom thou shalt see the Spirit descending, and remaining on him, the same is he which baptizeth with the Holy Ghost.*
>
> *And I saw, and bare record that this is the Son of God.*
>
> John 1:32-34

The water baptism John told the people of was a clean cut from the past; it was a new way. John had been with the circumcision lineage; now he was an outcast, for the new way was a breaking down of the old plan.

When they heard that cry, that awful cry of the Spirit, and the message he gave, "Repent, for the kingdom of heaven is at hand! Make straight paths for your feet, without treading down others or exalting undue rights" all were startled. They were awakened, thinking the Messiah had come. Their searching was tremendous! "Is this He? If not, who can it be?" they wondered.

John said, "I am a voice crying, making a way for Messiah to come."

> *And this is the record of John, when the Jews sent priests and Levites from Jerusalem to ask him, Who art thou?*
>
> *And he confessed, and denied not; but confessed, I am not the Christ.*
>
> *And they asked him, What then? Art thou Elias? And he saith, I am not. Art thou that prophet? And he answered, No. ..*
>
> *...I am the voice of one crying in the wilderness, Make straight the way of the lord, as said the prophet Esaias.*
>
> John 1:19-23

The Cry Brings Conviction

"Individual purging/purposing," he cried out, "must be in your life!" God's Word came forth through him:

> *...the rough ways shall be made smooth;*
>
> *And all flesh shall see the salvation of God.*
>
> *Then said he to the multitude that came forth to be baptized of him, O generation of vipers, who hath warned you to flee from the wrath to come?*
>
> *Bring forth therefore fruits worthy of repentance, and begin not to say within yourselves, We have Abraham*

to our father...God is able of these stones to raise up children unto Abraham.

And now also the ax is laid unto the root of the trees: every tree therefore which bringeth not forth good fruit is hewn down, and cast into the fire.

And the people asked him, saying, What shall we do then?...

...And he said unto them, Do violence to no man, neither accuse any falsely; and be content with your wages.

Luke 3:5-10, 14

God was pressing life through him. God was moving the multitude and changing the situation at hand through him. The banks of the Jordan were covered, *filled*, with people, and the conviction upon the people was tremendous. The multitude cried out and were baptized of John in the Jordan, confessing their sins.

Oh, to be alone with God! John had been alone in the wilderness, and he heard the Word of God, which had power to change those around him.

...the word of God came unto John the son of Zacharias in the wilderness.

And he came...preaching the baptism of repentance for the remission of sins.

Luke 3:2, 3

Alone—oh, to be alone with God so we can get His mind and thought, His impression and revelation of the need of the people!

Alone! Alone!
   Jesus bore it all alone;
 He gave Himself to save His own;
   He suffered, bled, and died alone.

A Burden Births the Cry

There was nothing ordinary about John; all was extraordinary. He was unafraid to cry out God's message of repentance to anyone, regardless of his rank or position. King Herod was reproved by him because of his sinful relationship with Herodias, his brother Philip's wife, and for all the evils which Herod had done. (See Luke 3:19.) Even John's death was not ordinary. Herodias' daughter danced before Herod, who promised her up to half of his kingdom. She asked for John the Baptist's head.

Yes, this holy man was alone. God had John in such a sanctified, separated way that he would express that cry, the burden for the whole land. He would cry for the sins of the people, "God is holy! We are the children of Abraham, the children of faith! Awful judgment is coming!"

Cry, cry—he could not help but do it, because of their sin. John had been filled with the Holy Ghost from his mother's womb. He had the burden of the Spirit in him.

John was stern, but the land was still open to Jesus. Jesus walked in a way they knew; John came in a new way. John came neither eating nor drinking; he came crying. The only place he could breathe and be free was in the wilderness, the atmosphere of heaven, where he turned with a message to declare the preparation needed— repentance before Jesus came—to open the place of redemption.

The Spirit's Cry to You

The cry of the Spirit to you today is:

- *Allow a working of the Spirit in you, then allow God to work through you for others.* Remember John: his father and mother left behind; his heart bleeding at the altar; his soul bearing the burden, the cry, the need of people.
- *Give way unto the Lord, even to the operation of the Spirit.* Be a people known of God, doing exploits, and gripped by God.
- *Continue in the things revealed unto thee,* and so the enemy will be put to flight. Even those around thee shall acknowledge, "The Lord has blessed!"

(Wales, August 1925)

Chapter 3

Divine Charging

If you will believe, you shall see the salvation of God. ONLY BELIEVE!

Believe there is something to bring us into the kingdom of God—out of a natural order, into a divine order with divine power for promotion, in which we are changed by the power of God by Another who is greater than we are. Scripture says:

> *He came unto his own, and his own received him not.*
> *But as many as received him, to them gave he power to become the sons of God....*

> John 1:11, 12

We are in a great place when we have no one to turn to but God. Having only God to help us, we are in a great place. For there, God will change the situation that has bound us. Who will do it? *"Not I, but Christ,"* Paul reminds us (Galatians 2:20).

A new divine order for us to come into awaits us. It is a divine place where GOD works the miracle. But God waits for us to act. We must turn to Him.

Some boilers are made to go off at a 10-pound pressure, some at a 250-pound pressure, and some at a 350-pound pressure. What pressure, or problem, do you want to blow off today? God will help you in your problem. Only believe. All things are possible. Only believe.

> *But ye shall receive power, after that the Holy Ghost is come upon you.*

> Acts 1:8

What is there for us in this mighty baptism of the Holy Ghost? With it we can be so moved by the power until Llarelly and the whole of South Wales feel the power of God again. The people shall know their great inheritance in Christ Jesus. All shall know we have been with Jesus, who changes them.

It was that way when people met with Jesus, and we are bone of His bone and flesh of His flesh. And He has given us of His Spirit, grace for grace. Jesus was full of grace, filled with the power of the Spirit. He, through the Holy Ghost, gave to man grace. In Him the Trinity was manifest, promising a power like His. He was in agony, but the work had to continue. Those He left behind were to be likewise clothed, charged with divine power by the divine working of the Spirit. Now we today are baptized into the same Spirit. We are partakers of the divine nature, living in a divine changing, with our whole being aflame with the same passion that Jesus had.

It Will Never Stop!

You would have thought this wonderful baptism in the Spirit would quiet the disciples down. On the contrary! It reminds me of the first engine. When Stephenson got it all ready, he was excited for his sister Mary to see it. When Mary saw it, she said, "John, it will never go. It will never go!"

Stephenson said to his sister, "Get in." She got in and he pressed a button. *The engine went.* She said, "Oh, John! Oh, John, it will never stop! It will never stop!"

As the disciples waited and prayed in the Upper Room, it looked as if the baptism would never come. But it did come, and now we know it will never stop! But they had the sense to wait until it did come.

What do I think when I see people still waiting for the Holy Ghost? Beloved, I believe it is wrong to wait for the Holy Ghost. *The Holy Ghost is waiting for US.* The Holy Ghost has come, and He will not leave until the Church goes to be with her Lord forevermore. When I see people waiting, I know something is wrong.

The Holy Ghost begins to reveal uncleanness, judging hardness of heart and all impurity to men. Until the process of cleansing is complete, the Holy Ghost is not welcome in them. But when the bodies are clean, sanctified, Jesus delights to fill them with His Holy Spirit.

I know it will never stop!

We are wholly God's in the Holy Ghost's process of cleansing and preparing our bodies to be a temple for the Spirit; to be made like unto Him. It is the will of God, even your sanctification, that you should be filled into all the fullness of God, like a bannered army clothed upon with Him. The Trinity is like dynamite flowing through you, working holy, mighty power within the human frame.

God means for us to be in His divine order—swallowed up in Him and then receiving a new body, a new mind, a new tongue. No man can tame the tongue; but God, by the Holy Ghost, can change the whole body, including the tongue, to a perfect position. The divine order is a divine cooperation—we allow Christ to become enthroned within us .

Divine Power Within

Acts 1:8 says that you shall receive power when the Holy Ghost comes upon you in His perfect, operative, divine adjustment. The sanctification of the Spirit causes an unfolding of the divine plan— here is the hallmark of the mystery of divine ability, which must come in our day in its fullness. If you have the Holy Ghost, you have divine ability and power. Jesus was anointed with the Holy Ghost and went about doing good, for God was in Him bodily, in all fullness (Acts 10:38).

I see, I know, the divine order. We must press into the fullness of it. We are to speak of what we know and testify of what we have seen, the Holy Ghost being our witness.

I see the Master in His royal robe of holiness, an impregnation of love, moving and acting in the present tense of divine power. It is an association to be imparted to us. "*Ye*" shall receive power, according to Acts 1:8.

The Master was in Acts 1:8. The disciples had to come into it. We are in it, of it, into it. And we cannot get rid of it, once this power-divine is in us.

It is a tremendous thing to be born into this by God. It is a serious thing. Yes, once engrafted, it is a serious thing to grieve the Holy Ghost. The baptism of the Holy Ghost is a fearful place if we are not going on with God, for great is our conviction of sin.

The Holy Ghost comes to *abide*. God must awake us to our responsibility: to live an inbreathed *life* of power. We can never be the same after the Holy Ghost has come upon us! Full of the Spirit, we must be instant in season and out of season, always abounding, always full of the life of God, ready for every emergency!

I know the Lord laid His hand on me.
I know the Lord laid His hand on me;
He filled me with the Holy Ghost.
I know the Lord laid his hand on me.

Shout! The Victory Is Yours!

I am always, *always* in a place that is greater than the position and the need of the place. The baptism of the Holy Ghost is given to prepare us for acting when two ways meet. Only GOD can give us the decision we need of which way to go. Only He can bring off the victory we need. We simply stand still and see the salvation of God.

It's a great place! It's great to reach such a place of dignity, being able to shout unto God when the walls are up and it looks as if all would fail.

Shout! Shout! The victory is yours! The victory is yours! It's not to come at some future time; the victory is yours!

As you shout with a voice of triumph, the ensign will arise and the walls will fall. You will walk in and possess the city. It's a designed position. It is not of your making; it's a rising position, honoring the cry of the Master: *"It is finished,"* not "It is to BE finished" (John 19:30).

"It is finished"—God can make manifest that position as we are loyal to His divine purposes.

It is no little thing to be baptized with the Holy Ghost and to be saved from the power of Satan unto God. It is a greater thing than moving Mount Sinai for Him to change a nature from an earthly position to a heavenly desire! Oh, to be in the divine order!

Beloved, Jesus was in the perfect order. He began to do and teach. He began to be. He lived in a "know." We, too, must live in a "know." God has declared it: We must be living epistles of Christ, *known* and read of all men (2 Corinthians 3:2). We are to have *knowledge* of Him through His Word, which abides in our hearts. It is a Word of activity, a Word of power—the same power we received when the Holy Ghost came upon us and made us witnesses in Jerusalem, Judaea, Samaria, and the uttermost parts of the earth.

"The Lord Will Make a Way!"

How do you walk in the kingdom of the Master? *By compassion that faileth not*, that sees when no other sees, that feels when no other feels. It's a divine compassion. It comes by the Word, for the Master is the Word of God. We are balanced on God's side according to our faith. Scripture says, *"Who is he that overcometh the world, but he that believeth Jesus is the Son of God?"* (1 John 5:5). Our life of faith is in Another, in our association with Another. Our faith is in the Master. We are living only for Him; therefore, He can extend Himself through us. He is taking the lead through us.

Very early one morning, I was traveling in Sweden. An old lady came into the railway carriage, leaning on her daughter's arm. She sat down. Her face was so full of anguish, I was disturbed. I could not rest. I said to my interpreter, "What is the cause of that woman's trouble? I want to know."

The dear old lady said, "I am over seventy. I had hoped to carry my body through, but gangrene has set in my legs. I am on my way to the hospital to have my legs off, and the pain is terrible. I do not want to have my legs off at my age."

I was bound to tell her Jesus could heal her. Her face lit up. Her eyes sparkled. She became radiant with hope.

Then the train stopped. The carriage filled up with workmen, who stood between me and the woman. It looked hopeless for further talk. A big man stood right between us. The devil said, "Now you are done."

Jesus knew how to answer the devil when He walked the earth. He answered him with the Word of God. The devil may leave a dead fish, but not a *live* one!

The devil said, "Now you are done."

I said, "No! My Lord will make a way" (Isaiah 43:19).

Just then, the big man stretched his legs out. I put my hand on the woman and said, "In the Name of Jesus, I bind and loose this woman."

The man did not know what had happened, but God knew. At that moment, she was healed.

What is my object in telling this story? Acts 1:8 (paraphrased) says, "You will receive POWER after the Holy Ghost comes upon you." Jesus was clothed upon with power and with a ministry of *imparting* the power emblematic of divinity, with an installation that never fails. You have received power to breathe in life and scatter the power of the enemy, and nothing shall by any means hurt you!

When the train stopped, the old lady began to get out of the carriage. The daughter said, "Why, Mother?"

The lady said, "I am going back home. I am healed." As long as the train stood still, she walked up and down past the carriage window. She said to the interpreter, "I am going home. I am healed."

> *He'll never forget to keep me,*
> *He'll never forget to keep me.*
> *My Father has many dear children;*
> *But He'll never forget to keep me.*

Glory Is Risen Upon Thee

God will not allow those who trust in Him to become failures in the straightened place. *God* will do the work. Yes, He can do it. His Word is a living Word of divine activity with momentum. It has power to change the nature of things by the power of the Spirit. God the Holy Ghost can take the Word of Jesus and breathe into the hearer, quickening his spirit. All disease and weakness must go at the rebuke of the Master. And God enables us to speak and bind the enemy and set the captive free.

Beloved, arise! The glory of the Lord is risen upon thee, empowering life into thy weakness. God is not making thee the tail but the head (Deuteronomy 28:13). This is a wonderful day, filled with the Spirit, the breath of the Almighty!

Jesus began to *do*, then to teach. You are in a divine process, with revelation and divine power in the place of *manifestation*. If I only come to impart the life which has brought revelation, God will be with me and blessings will flow.

One day on a busy car route in New York, I saw a great crowd. I asked the driver to stop. I saw a boy lying in the agony of death. I said, "What is it, boy?"

He answered in a breathless voice, "Cramp."

There was no time to pray—only to act! (I see Acts 1:8 in this, which says, *"Ye shall receive power"* is the divine order.) I felt fire burning, power flowing, divine glory! Getting my hand around the boy, I said, "Come out!"

The boy jumped up and ran off, never even saying, "Thank you."

Another day, I had risen early on board ship and was on deck. I saw a man; he did not see me. He seemed to be in great pain. I heard him say, "Oh, I cannot bear it. What shall I do?"

I jumped up and said, "Come out!"

He said, "What is it?!"

I said, "It's God!"

The man had hurt his back lifting a heavy weight. Now he was healed.

Yes, beloved, we have a mighty God. He is able to help, able to comfort. He is the God of all comfort.

With the power of impartation to a needy world, be active, for you have renewed power. You have the power of changing. When the Holy Ghost has come upon you, God is glorified and the need of the needy is met. Power received goes forth, and God is glorified!

After receiving the power, let the rivers flow. (See John 7:37.) Amen.

(South Wales, August 1925)

Chapter 4

How To Understand Voices

Beloved, believe not every spirit, but try the spirits whether they are of God: because many false prophets are gone out in the world.

Hereby know ye *the Spirit of God:* Every *spirit that confesseth that Jesus Christ is come in the flesh is of God:*

And every spirit that confesseth not that Jesus Christ is come in the flesh is not of God: and this is that spirit of antichrist, whereof ye *have heard that it should come; and even now already is it in the world.*

Ye are of God, little children, and have overcome them: because greater is he that is in you, than he that is in the world.

They are of the world: therefore speak they of the world, and the world heareth them.

We are of God: he that knoweth God heareth us; he that is not of God heareth not us. Hereby know we the spirit of truth, and the spirit of error.

Beloved, let us love one another: for love is of God; and every one that loveth is born of God, and knoweth God.

He that loveth not knoweth not God; for God is love.

In this was manifested the love of God toward us, because that God sent his only begotten Son into the world, that we might live through him.

1 John 4:1-9

Many voices are sounding in the world. We read it is so in First Corinthians 14. I want you to be able to understand voices—to discern spirit *voices*—and to know exactly what the Scripture says about them.

I know a great many people are great on Conan Doyle, who, you will find, is trying to delve into mysteries.[1] Now, there is nothing mystic about our business; and I want to tell everybody who comes to our meetings, you will have no share with us if you have anything to do with spiritism. We denounce it as being of the devil, and we don't want fellowship with you. If you want to join up with both good and evil, the devil will be the one who gets you at the finish.

Let me tell you what you will be getting yourself involved with: not the spirit of lawlessness, but *"...the spirit that now worketh in the children of disobedience"* (Ephesians 2:2). It is a spirit of disobedience. It is the *"...spirit of antichrist, ...and even now already is in the world"* (1 John 4:3). It is right in the midst of things today. Spiritism, mysticism, Christian Science—they are all akin. None of them obey God and make room for the blood, and you cannot get near God but by the blood. It is impossible. The blood of

---

1 Sir Arthur Conan Dayle (1859-1930) was a British physician and detective-story writer. His mysteries introduced the world to the fictitious detective Sherlock Holmes.

Jesus Christ is the only power that can make a clear road into the kingdom of God for you.

Beloved, you have to be in a position to *"...try the spirits whether they are of God"* (1 John 4:1). Why should you try them? Try the spirits to see whether they are of God for this reason: to be able to discern the true revelation. And the true revelation which will come to you will always sanctify the heart. It will never have an "if" in it. When the devil came to Jesus, he had an "if." He said, *"IF thou be the Son of God..."* and *"...IF thou wilt fall down and worship me"* (Matthew 4:3,9).

The Holy Ghost never comes with an "if." He comes with something that is strong and sure. He is the divine oratory of the wonderful Word of God. The mystic Conan Doyle's position, however, is satanic.

The Blood Has Power!

One day I was walking along a street in Bradford and met one of my friends. He was a man who lived in the Spirit. I said to him. "Friend, where are you going?"

He replied, "I have a big job on tonight."

"What is it?"

"Oh, there is a spiritualistic seance tonight, and I'm going."

"Don't you think it is dangerous? I don't think it's wise for believers to go to such places," I said.

"I am led to go, to test it according to Scripture," he replied.

(Beloved, I advise you not to go to these places.) My friend went and sat down in the midst of the meeting. The medium began to try to take control. My friend did not speak, but just keep himself under the blood, whispering the preciousness of the blood of Jesus.

After trying for some time to get things under control, the leader said, "We can do nothing tonight. There is somebody who believes in the blood."

Hallelujah! Do you believe in the blood, beloved? You should!

I often have dealt with people under the influence of evil powers, people in fits and such. Sometimes I have come across people so much controlled by evil powers that, every time they wanted to speak, the evil powers spoke. It is a very dangerous matter, but it is true: People get possessed with the devil .

The man in the tomb that the New Testament speaks about, was terribly afflicted with evil powers and cut himself with stones and strong cords night and day. There he was, in the tomb, crying out. Jesus came on the scene, and those evil powers caused the man to run. As soon as the man got in front of Jesus, the evil spirits in him said, *"...I adjure thee by God, that thou torment me not"* (Mark 5:7).

This man had no power to get free, yet these evil spirits were still so troubled in the presence of Jesus that they cried out, "Don't torment me!"

They resisted Jesus, but He set the man free! Oh, thank God for Jesus! I want you to know that Jesus wants you to be so under His power, so controlled by and filled with the Holy Ghost, that the power of authority in you will resist all evil! This is an important thing for believers to know, because many believers are not on their guard against the devil.

I want to impress another fact upon your mind: Every believer should reach a place in the Holy Ghost where *he has no desire except the desire of God.* The Holy Ghost has to possess us till we are filled and led—yes, divinely led—by Him. And it is a mighty thing to be filled with the Holy Ghost!

Tongues Interpretation

The Lord—He is the mighty power of government, for the Scripture says, "The government shall be upon His shoulders." And now He has taken US on His shoulders; therefore, let Him lead you where He will.

Be Led by Jesus, Not Impressions

Don't you want to be led by Jesus? If He leads you, He will lead you into truth, into nothingness (but when you are in nothingness, you will be in power), and into weakness (but when you are in weakness, God will be with you in might and everything that would seem of weakness of the human side will be under the control of divine power).

Now I want to deal with a very important matter. I have people by the hundreds who are continually pressing on me with their difficulties and their desires—their holy and noble, yet *strange*, desires. These people are where two ways meet, and they do not know which way to take. Some have impressions of what they should do. But I will show you what becomes of impressions.

A woman came to me one day and said, "Oh, the Spirit of the Lord was mighty upon me this morning."

I said, "Good!"

"Oh, I want to tell you about it. I want you to tell me if there is such a place as Ingerow anywhere near here."

I answered, "Yes, there is."

"Well, that place has been upon my heart. I have to go and preach there."

There is nothing wrong with that, is there? But then I asked, "What is the message?"

"I don't exactly know."

"Now, come—what is the message?" I asked.

"Oh, I have to speak to someone about their soul."

"And you don't know there is such a place? The place is toward Skipton," I replied.

"But I have to go."

"Now, come—I want you to think," I said. "You are working, are you not? Do you think anybody in the mill will commend you going to a place you don't know, to speak to someone you don't know?"

Was it of God? That is the first thing to ask. No, it was an impression of a desire to "be something." That's dangerous!

My daughter tried to stop her, but she went the first chance she got. She arrived at the station. Nobody was there for her to give a message to. What resulted? She was soon in an asylum.

She had been led by an impression. Now I'm going to tell you of another lady, who was led in a different way: by the Word of God. She came to me yesterday and said, "The Spirit of the Lord is upon me. I have to preach the Gospel."

I said, "There is nothing wrong in that."

She said, "I want to know where I have to go. I have come to you to see if the Lord has told you where I have to go."

I immediately knew what to say. I said, "Yes, you have to begin at home. Begin at 'Jerusalem.' If you are successful, go to 'Judaea.' Then if you are successful there, God will send you to the uttermost parts of the world. But God is not going to send you to the uttermost parts of the world until you have been successful 'round about Jerusalem.'" (See Acts 1:8.)

Today we have a tremendously big job: reaching the world. It is well worth doing, and I want to do it well.

I want to tell you how to tell the difference between the right and the wrong way to follow. The Scriptures and the Holy Ghost will show you. They have wisdom; they will keep you from being foolish. The Scriptures, for instance, showed that lady I spoke of where to preach the Gospel. And the Holy Ghost, having perfect insight into knowledge, wisdom, and truth, always gives you balance so you won't go overboard on something that is not of God.

To walk in the right way, you have to have one thing removed from your life: fear. If fear is removed, power and confidence will come in its place. You also have to have something that must remain: love. You must love to obey God rather than to obey your inclinations to "be something." (But if God wants to make you someone, that is different.)

My wife tried her best to make me someone. She could not do it. Her heart, her love, her desire were right, for she did her best to make me a preacher. She used to say, "Now, father, you could do it if you would. I want you to preach next Sunday."

I tried everything to get ready. I don't know what I did not try. It would be best not to tell you what I tried. I had as many notes as would suit a parson for a week! But when I got up to preach, I gave out my text and then said, "If anybody can preach, now is your chance, for I am done."

That did not take place once, but many times. She was determined and I was willing. But it was the little children that I could take right in. I could teach them while my wife preached, and I was pleased to do it.

But when the Holy Ghost came on me, *then* I was ready. *Then* the preaching abilities were not mine but the Lord's. To be filled with the Holy Ghost is to be filled with divine equipment. It must be ALL for Jesus! Oh, I tell you, whether you believe it or not, there is nothing good without Jesus in the whole thing!

You could jump on this platform and confidently say that you are right about something. But when you have no confidence, Jesus is all the confidence you need!

God must have men and women in His Church who are on fire for Him. Are you on fire for God? If you are, God will mightily send you forth in the unction of the Spirit, and sinners will feel condemned. But it will never be accomplished if you have in your mind that you are going to "be something." The baptism is a baptism of death, and you are to live only unto God.

Let God Be Manifested, Not You

I want to tell you about one of the most trying things with which I have had to deal. I have had many trying things to deal with—people have asked me all kinds of things, and I have had to examine their positions carefully to see what God has for them. I will relate a story along these lines which cannot but help you.

Is there anything wrong with wanting to be the best missionary in the world? Not at all! And yet...

Two young women worked as telegraph operators. One of them had offered herself to God for the mission field. She was a beautiful girl, full of purity, truth, and righteousness. She had a lovely countenance; her expression alone could do wonderful things to others for God. A voice came to her.

Oh, beloved, try the voices. Try the spirits.

A voice came to her and said, "I will make you the mightiest missionary in the world."

That was exactly what she wanted! It was her heart's desire. She was so moved within by this! "And I will find you all the money you want," the voice said.

She became very excited about it. But her sister sensed that there was something "out of place." She went to the head person at work and said, "Could my sister and I have an hour off from work?" and got her sister and herself free.

The voice came with such tremendous force to her sister that *she could not let it go.*

Try the spirits. God will never do anything like that girl experienced; He will never send you an unreasonable, unmanageable message you "can't let go of."

The devil said, "Don't tell anybody."

That's the devil's way. Anything that is holy can be told on the housetops. We have no secrets given to us from God that we cannot share. All the secrets worth having are worth telling. If we cannot tell them, they are not worth having. God wants us to be able to tell ALL.

Then the voice came again. "You might take your sister with you," it said. "I want you at the station tonight. You will find that a train will come into the station at 7:32. After you have bought your ticket, you will have a certain amount of change left. And in that train, you will see a woman wearing a nurse's bonnet. On the other side will be a man who has the money you want. When you get out at Glasgow, you can deposit the money in [a certain bank] at [a certain place]."

Here was a lack of presentation of thought. There were no banks open at seven-thirty—and investigation showed that there was *no* such bank in that place.

What did this message do? It got her ear. She paid so much attention to it that she paid no attention to anyone else.

I will tell you what the danger is: If you cannot be reasoned with, you are wrong. If you are right and everybody else is wrong, if you cannot bear examination, if what you hold cannot bear the light of the truth, I don't care who you are, you are wrong! It will save you a lot of trouble if you will just think about what others say. Don't say flatly, "Oh, I know. I KNOW I am the one who is right."

It is a very serious thing when nobody else knows but you. May God deliver you from such a condition, for it is not of Him, but of the flesh. There are two workings: the working of the Spirit and the working of the flesh. The working of the Spirit will always be contrary, to the working of the flesh.

We tried to console the woman, but nothing could be done. She *knew* it was the voice of the Lord.

The train came in at exactly 7:32. She said to her sister, "Now we know this is right."

The change was exactly as she had been told it would be. That was right. But the next thing was not right. When the train came in, there were no such characters as the voice had described; hence, she didn't get any money, much less all the money she wanted which the voice had promised.

Ah, evil voices—how shall we know whether they are of God? When God speaks, He speaks on the lines of wisdom.

Remember, when the devil came to Jesus, he said, *"... IF thou wilt fall down and worship me"* (Matthew 4:9). The devil knew this sin of worshipping him would eliminate Jesus from dying for man as the spotless Lamb of God. And Jesus knew how foolish his demand was. He wisely answered, *"... it is written, Thou shalt worship the Lord thy God, and him only shalt thou serve"* (Matthew 4:10).

In the story of these two young women, what was wrong? The wrong was that they ought to have judged the spirits. If the young women had asked, "Did Jesus come in the flesh?" the voice would have answered, "No." There is no satanic voice in the world, and no spiritualistic medium, who will acknowledge that Jesus came in the flesh. The devil never will, and he is the father of those spiritualistic mediums Conan Doyle included in his works. They speak foolishness and not wisdom.

When those evil spirits found that the woman they spoke to would do anything they wanted, they said, "We will make you the biggest missionary in the world AND get you all the money you want."

She should have known that wasn't of God. I have never known anything like that to be of God, and you never will in your life, either.

A man came to me once and said, "I have in my hands a certain food for invalids. It will bring in millions of pounds for the missionaries."

I said to him, "I will not have anything to do with it."

Things like that are not a success. God does not work that way. If God wanted you to have gold, He could rain it in your house. He has all the gold, and the cattle on a thousand hills are His (Haggai 2:8; Psalm 50:10).

Beloved, I want you to see that Jesus was the meekest man in the world. He had power to turn bread into gold, and yet He never did—except for somebody else. *When anybody preaches for the kingdom's sake, He will provide for him.*

Seek to be filled with the Holy Ghost for the people's sake. Seek only for God and the rain will fall. Power will be made manifest in your mortal body and you will have God's provision, if you are really in the Spirit.

Were the two young women I spoke of delivered? Yes, and they have been used in China for many years. Thank God, there is a way out when we have made a mistake!

This is an important word. I am saying everything I can by the grace of God and the revelation of the Spirit to make you careful and yet careless. Be careful of satanic powers. Be careless (have no cares about your abilities, personal desires, needs, or problems) when the power of God is upon you with unction force, so He will be manifested, *and not you.*

Glorify God, Not Man

Is there anything wrong with the story I am going to tell you? I want you to pay attention and see.

Quite a lot of people at York had been saved in the marketplace. One of the young men that had been gathered into the kingdom soon exhibitted abilities for being a wonderful teacher. He led the people forth triumphantly in the morning meetings. Everybody was lifted up in joy because of his teaching and preaching abilities.

When I went there, the power of the Spirit fell upon us. Straightaway, many people were under the power of God, including that young man. When everyone saw him laid out under the power of the Spirit, they said, "Oh, Brother Wigglesworth, we have got one of the finest young men here. For him to be filled with the Holy Ghost means we will have the greatest teacher in the world!"

The leaders came and said they were overjoyed at what was happening. I said, "Be still. The Lord will do His own work."

In a short time, he was through in the Spirit. Everybody began to rejoice and applaud. They all came to him and shook his hand, saying, "Now we have the greatest teacher there is."

Was it wrong for them to rejoice at a move of the Holy Ghost upon the man? It was perfectly right—and yet it was the most wrong thing they could have done. That's when they fell into great error. They should not have applauded him. It's as surely of the devil as anything that ever happened to anybody. God has never yet allowed any human body to be applauded. Oh, I do pray God will save you from doing that same thing. I hope you would not hear my words and say, "Oh, Brother Wigglesworth, you did preach well today!"

The people should have quietly been thankful in their hearts, in their thoughts. The devil never knows your thoughts; and if you won't let your thoughts out in public, you will be safe. He may give you a thought of evil or even many thoughts of evil, but that is not sin. All these things come from without; but they can't get within you unless you invite them. The devil can suggest evil things for you to receive; but if you are pure, his suggestions will be like water on a duck's back.

What happened next at the meeting? The people said, "I should not wonder if you were a second John the Baptist."

They really were elated with him. The young man tried to throw it off and keep well balanced when he saw what was coming at him. But the devil came with a voice as loud as a cannon: "Don't you know, you ARE John the Baptist."

Still, he threw it off.

Listen, it was the *believers* who first told him he may be a second John the Baptist. After that, the devil never let him alone about it. "You are surely John the Baptist," he'd say. "There is no person in the world like you. *Arise, John the Baptist!*"

At eight o'clock in the morning, that young man went down the street, crying out, "I am John the Baptist!"

Oh, if the saints had only kept from applauding him! That was the work of the devil.

Pray, *"Lord bring us to a place of humility and brokenheartedness, where we will see the danger of satanic powers."*

Don't believe the devil is a big, ugly monster; he comes as an angel of light. He comes at a time when you have done well and tells you about it. He comes to make you feel you are "somebody." The devil is an exalted demon. Take heed, lest at his leading you covet exaltation of self and fall into deception and pride.

Oh, look at the Master! If you could see Him as I see Him sometimes: rich, and yet He became poor; in glory, yet He took upon Himself the form of a servant. Yes, a servant—that is the Lord.

Have you read the beatitudes in the Word of God? God gave them to us so we will be broken, humble, and in the dust. From there *He* will exalt us. God will raise us up and put us in a high place!

(New Zealand, January 15, 1924)

Chapter 5

We Mean Business With God

But a certain man named Ananias, with Sapphira his wife, sold a possession,

And kept back part of the price, his wife also being privy to it, and brought a certain part, and laid it at the apostles' feet.

But Peter said, Ananias, why hath Satan filled thine heart to lie to the Holy Ghost, and to keep back part of the price of the land?

Whiles it remained, was it not thine own? and after it was sold, was it not in thine own power? why hast thou conceived this thing in thine heart? thou hast not lied unto man, but unto God.

And Ananias hearing these words fell down, and gave up the ghost: and great fear came on all them that heard these things.

And the young men arose, wound him up, and carried him out, and buried him.

And it was about a space of three hours after; when his wife, not knowing what was done, came in.

And Peter answered unto her, Tell me whether ye sold the land for so much? And she said, Yea, for so much.

Then Peter said unto her, How is it that ye have agreed together to tempt the Spirit of the lord? behold, the feet of them which have buried thy husband are at the door, and shall carry thee out.

Then fell she down straightway at his feet, and yielded up the ghost: and the young men came in, and found her dead, and, carrying her forth, buried her by her husband.

And great fear came upon all the church, and upon as many as heard these things.

And by the hands of the apostles were many signs and wonders wrought among the people; (and they were all with one accord in Solomon's porch.

And of the rest durst no man join himself to them: but the people magnified them.

And believers were the more added to the lord, multitudes both of men and women.)

Insomuch that they brought forth the sick into the streets, and laid them on beds and couches, that at the least the shadow of Peter passing by might overshadow some of them.

There came also a multitude out of the cities round about unto Jerusalem, bringing sick folks, and them which were vexed with unclean spirits: and they were healed every one.

Acts 5:1-16

Only believe. Only believe!

Believe that there is power in God's Word which brings life where death is. Jesus said that the time would come when the dead would hear the voice of the Son of Man and live (John 5:25). Believe this Word, for *"...all things are possible to him that believeth"* (Mark 9:23).

The life of the Son is in the Word. All who are saved realize this. They know that this Word frees from death and corruption. Jesus brought life, and immortality to life, through the Gospel. We can never exhaust the Word—the life in it is abundant!

The Word says that there is a river, the streams of which make glad the city of God (Psalm 46:4). Its source is in the glory. The essence of its life is God. The life of Jesus embodied is its manifested power.

Jesus Himself had died and given us the victory. The victorious Son of God in humanity overcometh! He gave up His life for the needy. Immortality, produced in mortality, has changed the situation of death and defeat for us. This is life indeed, and the end of death: *Christ*, who brought life, and immortality to life, through the Gospel.

No Lie in the Church!

This is a wonderful subject. It is wonderful because of its manifestation in the Church. No lie could live in God's first Church. The new Church the Holy Ghost is building has no lie, either; only purity and holiness unto the Lord.

I see that the new Church established in the breath of God is working in a supernatural way, making faces shine with His glory.

Men are so like God—loving right, hating iniquity, fearing evil—that a lie is *unable* to remain in their midst.

It is a lie that there is condemnation for you. No man can condemn you. Many may try, but God's Word says, "Who is he that condemneth—Christ that died?" (Romans 8:34, paraphrased). Will Jesus condemn the sheep for whom He died? He died to save men, and He saves all who believe.

God is purifying our hearts by faith. God has come forth to us in His Church, clothing us with His Spirit's might. We are living in the blaze of this glorious day. It is glorious because there is nothing greater than the Gospel!

Acts 5 says that Ananias and Sapphira were moved to bring an offering to the Church. (The first day was a measure; *the latter day is to be MORE glorious.* The day will come when we will offer *all*. We will count *nothing* our own, because we shall be so taken up with the Lord! The Church will be ripened unto coming glory.)

The two sold a possession. It was their own, but when it was sold, it looked like there was a great deal. They reasoned, "The Pentecostal order is new. It might dry up."

They agreed to give a part and reserve the rest of the money for themselves, saying they were giving all. Satan is subtle. Many miss the greatest things by rationalizing and drawing aside from the commitments God wants them to make. Let us pay our vows unto the Lord!

Peter said, "Ananias, why hath Satan filled thine heart to lie to the Holy Ghost?" The moment Ananias lied to the Holy Ghost, he was smitten. Sapphira died, too, when she lied. God has shown us in this Holy Ghost baptism a new order of the Spirit. He does not want lies of the devil in the Church.

One day when I came into my house, my wife said, "Did you come in the front door?"

I said, "No, I came in the back ."

"Oh, at the front you would have seen a crowd," she said, "and a man with little clothing on. He is crying out, 'I have committed the unpardonable sin!'"

As I went to the front door, God whispered to me, *This is what I baptized you in the Spirit for.*

The man came in and cried, "I have committed the unpardonable sin."

I said, "You lying devil, come out in Jesus' Name!"

He said, "What is it? I am free. Thank God, I never did commit that sin!"

No man living has committed the unpardonable sin, for the good and the evil are preserved until the Holy Ghost is withdrawn from the world. We are all in a good place of pardon, kept by the power of God.

Great fear came upon the Church because of what happened to Ananias and Sapphira. The people had a love that fears to grieve God. They could ask and get anything from Him, for they were in one accord and perfect love, fidelity, oneness, and consolation.

God was lifting the Church into a place of manifested reconciliation, of oneness of accord, so the devil would have no power in the people's midst, and God could have cause to smile on them all the time.

"And by the hands of the apostles were many signs and wonders wrought among the people..." (Acts 5:12). This verse shows that

purity of life before God brings manifested power among men, with multitudes being gathered into the kingdom.

God has mightily blessed the work of evangelism through men. If you are still lingering outside the kingdom, yield to God today. Get clean hands and a right purpose, and join that which is holy and on fire.

Mean business for God.

"And believers were the more added to the Lord, multitudes both of men and women" (Acts 5:14). Oh, for the kind of revival in Acts 5: God breaking forth everywhere! May London be swept by the power of God! There must be a great moving among us, a oneness of heart and soul, and it will surely be as God moves upon the people! We see this is so as we read these verses from Acts 5 again:

> *Insomuch that they brought forth the sick into the streets, and laid them on beds and couches, that at the least the shadow of Peter passing by might overshadow some of them.*
>
> *There came also a multitude out of the cities round about unto Jerusalem, bringing sick folks, ...and they were healed every one.*
>
> Acts 5:15, 16

Of One Mind and Heart

Every time, the effect of oneness of accord is the working of the oracle, the Word. Glory to God! It is so lovely!

The people had such a living faith in Acts 5, being of one heart and one mind, they thought, *Oh, if only Peter's shadow would pass over me, I would be healed!*

"What things soever ye desire, when ye pray, only believe" (Mark 11:24). GOD WILL DO IT! Have faith. God will heal the land. Oneness of heart and mind on the part of the Church means signs and wonders will be in all lands.

Beloved, I see we need to get more love, and then the Lord will do these things. How the Master can move among the needy and perishing when He has the right of way in the Church!

But not all will be rosy. There will be persecution, but the finest thing is persecution. We must have a ministry which makes the people glad and the devil mad. Never mind if the people run away from you when you tell them the Gospel, for conviction is in them and God has them.

And even if the people are glad, the Lord has them. It works both ways. Don't be disturbed at anything. Just let the Lord's will consume your life. Remember, it was written of the Master, "The zeal for thine house hath eaten Me up!" (John 2:17, paraphrased).

His was a melting, moving, broken condition—the poor One making many rich; having nothing, and yet possessing all things! Let us be in harmony with this divine plan, having knowledge cemented with love. Death to the old must have a perfect place in us, so that the life-power can be manifested.

First Things First

I once went to preach at some weekend meetings. When I arrived that Saturday night, it was snowing hard. A man stood at the door of the hall, laden with parcels. As we walked home afterwards, I said at the first lamppost we came to, "Brother, are you baptized in the Holy Ghost? Say you will be tonight."

As we went along, at every lamppost (nearly a hundred), I repeated the question. "Say you will be baptized tonight."

(I'm sure that he began wishing I would not be staying at his house.) At last we reached the gate to his yard. I jumped over it and said, "Now, you don't come in here unless you say you will be baptized with the Holy Ghost tonight."

"Oh, I feel so funny," he said, "but I will say it."

We went in. I asked his wife, "Are you baptized in the Holy Ghost?"

She said, "Oh, I want to be, but supper is ready. Come and eat."

I said, "No supper until you are both baptized in the Holy Ghost!"

Did God answer? Oh, yes. Soon they were both speaking in tongues.

Now, I believe God will baptize *you* today. Put up your hands and ask Him to. Also, if you are seeking healing or salvation, ask for it. God will meet you—and *everyone* who asks. Amen.[2]

(June 4, 1926)

---

2   To receive salvation through Jesus Christ, pray, "Jesus, I believe You are Lord. I believe You died for me on the cross and rose from the grave to give me eternal life. Come into my life, Lord. Amen."

Chapter 6

This Grace

I want to repeat the words which are ringing through my heart as the real knowledge of truth: When we are filled with the joy of the Lord, there comes forth a glad "Praise the Lord!" David knew that, and he wished all the powers that had breath would praise the Lord.

It is a tragedy if there is not a divine spring within you, pressing forth praise. God wants you so much in the Spirit that your WHOLE LIFE is a praise. How my soul longs for you to catch fire!

Displays of Inward Flame

Four things which are emblematic and divinely ascertained, or revealed by the Lord, are: *fire, love, zeal,* and *faith*.

Fire—burning up intensely, making us full of activity on a new line with God.

Love—where there is nothing but pure, undefiled willingness, or yieldedness, which knows no sacrifice.

Zeal—being so much in the will and the mighty power of God, until we press beyond measure into that which pleases God.

Faith—that which laughs at impossibilities and cries, "It shall be done!"

May God make these things immediately real before our eyes and give us these emblematic displays of inward flame!

The Manifested Power of the Glory

Our message on the fifth chapter of Romans is meant to take us further into God. These messages have been dealing with the reception of the life and the nature of the Son of God. We have been seeing that the nature of the Son of God could be transmitted unto us by the Word and that the Spirit could fill the vessel until the Word could be made life.

As the Spirit went through the vessel, took the Word, and poured it into the body, the body would become quickened by the same nature of Jesus, with the same power over all weaknesses.

It is an incorruptible force, pressing through human order, *changing* human order, and bringing it to the place where it is resurrection life, eternal life, life quickened by the Spirit and changed from one state of grace to another—even from glory to glory.

Many people in these days are receiving a clear knowledge of an inward working of the power of the Spirit. It is not only quickening their mortal bodies, but also pressing into that same natural body an incorruptible power which is manifesting itself; thus, getting it ready for rapture.

The divine teaching of the Lord has revealed unto us that this is the inward life: the new man in the old man, the new nature in the old nature, the resurrection power in the dead form, the quickening of all, the divine order of God manifested in the human body. In us is the life and nature of the living Christ. In us is power over all death.

Do not be afraid to claim it. You have power over all sin; power over all disease. In the body, the Christ-life is forming, quickening, until every vestige of natural order is eaten up by the life divine.

The former law was of the natural man. Now the new law is of the life of the Spirit, or the manifestation of the new creation, which was Christ in us, the manifested power of the glory.

Glory is a manifestation of a divine nature in the human body. There is one special thought we should dwell on: *"like precious faith."* We have received "Like precious faith" of all that have passed through: Abraham—I say it with grace; Jesus—I say it with grace; the Father—I say it with grace; the Holy Ghost—I say it with grace.

All that the Father has, all that Jesus has, all that the Holy Ghost has, we have access into; we have a right into; we have an open door into. There is nothing that can keep us out of it!

Jesus Christ is the Alpha and the Omega for us, that we may know grace, favor, and mercy to lift us into, and so take us through every situation.

Lift us into what? Into grace and peace multiplied!

Grace and peace be multiplied unto you through the knowledge of God, and of Jesus our Lord.

2 Peter 1:2

Do you want grace multiplied today? Do you want peace multiplied? You have it here in Christ, if you dare to believe. We have access; we have a right to it.

According as his divine power hath given unto us all things that pertain unto life and godliness, through the knowledge of him that hath called us to glory and virtue:

Whereby are given unto us exceeding great and precious promises: that by these ye might be partakers of the divine nature....

2 Peter 1:3, 4

We have access into, the right to, the promises. Yea and Amen! We have the right to all the heirship which He has made us heirs of.

Now I want to go from that thought and read the fifth chapter of Romans.

Therefore being justified by faith, we have peace with God through our Lord Jesus Christ.

Romans 5:1

You are justified; you are being made at peace. And remember, the peace of God is different from any other peace. It passeth all understanding (Philippians 4:7). It takes you away from being disturbed, until you are not moved by earthly things. It is a deep peace, created by the knowledge of a living faith, which is the living principle of the foundation of all truth: Christ in us.

This is a manifestation of God in us, which is the glory, or the nature of the glory, or the transportation of the glory, or the power to transport the glory.

Christ in us, the hope, is the evidence of the glory.

A Grace of Access

I want you to see how rich you are.

> *By whom also* [that is, by the Lord Jesus Christ, or the nature] *we have access by faith into this grace wherein we stand, and rejoice in hope of the glory of God.*
>
> Romans 5:2

This is perhaps the greatest of all thoughts we have reached: *Faith has access through Jesus Christ into all the fullness of God.* It was by grace first. You were saved through grace. But now there is another grace: a grace of access, a grace of entering in, a grace of understanding the unfolding of the mystery, a grace which shall bring us into a place of the knowledge of God.

In Second Peter 1:1, we have a very special word which will help us here.

It is true that Jesus came to us in grace. He met us in need and transformed us by His power. It is right to say that now we have an inheritance within us. It is right to say it is uncorruptible and undefiled. We have a right to say it is filled with glory and virtue. We have a right to say we have the same nature as the Lord Jesus Christ.

The nature of His flesh? No—and yes. It is true, He was made in likeness of our sinful flesh and for sin, and condemned sin in the flesh. But there is a higher order now for us to walk in; a spiritual order, a divine order, a divine nature, a "super" nature, a holy nature, a nature of love, a nature of faith.

We have the nature of faith, the divine nature, the same nature as He was spiritually. *He* has committed to us *His* faith.

All human weaknesses in believers are spoiled when it is of a mixture. The same is true of faith. If your faith is not perfect, your victories are uncertain, your prayers have lost the anointing, your pressing into the kingdom of God is somewhat veiled, your personality of divine power to lay hold is hindered. Why? God comes to us, breathes into us a new life, and shows us we have access into this grace wherein we stand, so that we may have a new nature that has *no* variableness, neither shadow of turning, but believes *all* things, hopeth *all* things, and is *all* the time being changed!

Tongues Interpretation

It is the law of the life of the Spirit of Christ which is the hope, which is the glory in the hope, which is the revelation in the glory of the hope, which is filled with opening of keen perception of things above, where Christ is sitting at the right hand of God; where we see jointly the Father and the Son.

And so filled with purity of unmixed reality, faith rises. It changes its order. It lays hold and believes. It dethrones and stands fast to see the kingdom of God manifested!

Faith: The Power of Access

Faith is the power of access. I'm referring to unfeigned faith: faith that never has a mixture, faith which never wavers, faith which has audacity, faith which is purified, faith which is sensitive to the breath of God, faith which is the very nature of the Son of God, faith which came from the Author of faith.

With it, we become the very same as He: holy in act, daring to believe, resting assured, and seeing the mighty power of God made manifest through this living faith.

This is that which takes us in to claim all He has. Faith brings sight. By faith, the crooked are to be made straight; the lame are to leap with joy; the blind have to be made free.

God has finished creation; it is forever completed by the perfect work of our Lord. We are complete in Him, belonging to the living Head. We are His righteousness, born into and created for His purpose, that we might be in the world, over all the powers of the world!

This eighth chapter of Romans is one of those marvelous masterpiece chapters. Yet *all* of God's Word lifts. You can feel yourself being lifted by it. Gravitation is the only thing that causes you to remain! The Spirit lifts. The Word of incarnation moves. The life divine operates. The Spirit quickeneth.

You are being changed—being made right, being made ready—by regeneration.

Regeneration is one of the greatest words in the Scriptures. The Word of God is regenerating; the power of the Word is quickening into, out of, unto. Whatever you were this morning, you will never be as you were again. But as you were not, you have to be now. Nothing will move you so much as knowing what you were, so that you may be what you were not.

Believe it: God's plan, purpose, revelation is for us today, that we may leap gloriously!

Tongues Interpretation

The Lord's life is moving. The Lord's life is flowing. Put thy spirit into the joy of the breath, and let yourself go on the bosom of His love, to be transformed by all the Spirit-life from above.

And rejoice in hope of the glory of God.

Romans 5:2

The hope of the glory of all saints is what we are laying a foundation for in this study. The hope of the glory is: *You must know that you are going!* The great and mighty masterpiece of all is the great plan of Rapture.

It is the hope of the glory! It is the life divine! It is the peace of God! It is the enrichment of the soul! It is shed abroad in our hearts by the Holy Ghost!

The Holy Ghost is the manifestation of God's Son. The manifestation of the revelation of God's Son comes by the Holy Ghost. The Holy Ghost is always revealing Him to us as divine, as so uniquely divine that He is in power of overcoming, He is in power of purity, He is in power of rising all the time!

And the Holy Ghost is shed abroad in our hearts for the very purpose that we may know that that which is in us has to go on to development. It must not cease in development. The Holy Ghost is there for *creating* development, and for moving us out, as the Lord would have us to be.

For when we were yet without strength, in due time Christ died for the ungodly.

For scarcely for a righteous man will one die: yet peradventure for a good man some would even dare to die.

But God commendeth his love toward us, in that, while we were yet sinners, Christ died for us.

Much more then, being now justified by his blood, we shall be saved from wrath through him.

For if, when we were enemies, we were reconciled to God by the death of his Son, much more, being reconciled, we shall be saved by his life.

Romans 5:6-10

What Christ Did for You

We are saved by His life! Now that we have received salvation, God wants to open our eyes to understand what Christ really did for us. In due time, at the end of the weeks of the law, when there was no arm to save, when there was no hope, when law had failed, Christ took our place on the cross. He delivered us from all the powers of human weaknesses and failure, and so came to us in our sins. When we were in sin, Christ died for us.

In due time, at the end of failure, at the right moment, He died for us and delivered us from the power of the devil. He delivered us from death, sin, and the grave. And He gave us a hope of immortality through His life. We are saved by His life!

Jesus had eternal properties. Jesus had power to impart His eternal gifts. He is here *now* to do that. He has delivered us from the curse of the law and set us free to enjoy His blessings.

Oh, who loves the Gospel more than those who have been delivered by the Gospel!

What is the Gospel? *It is the power of God unto salvation.* It has power to bring immortality and life. Immortality and life are the nature of the Lord Jesus, and through this life in us we are delivered from all things and being prepared for the glorious hope of the coming of the Lord.

> *CHRIST arose, a victor over death's domain,*
>
> *He arose, forever with His saints to reign;*
>
> *HE arose! He arose!*
>
> *Hallelujah, Christ arose!*

What was it that arose? Christ's life. How did He rise? Out of death and over death *victorious.* And were we not planted with Him? Were we not risen with Him? Then the only thing that can happen is for us to be seated with Him. The past is under the blood; the whole thing is finished!

Atonement: At One-ment

Now as we are entering into another step of this divine order, the Lord will speak to us.

> *And not only so, but we also joy in God through our lord Jesus Christ, by whom we have now received the atonement.*

> Romans 5:11

Atonement means "at one-ment." *One-ment* is "perfect association." Whatever Christ's appointment was in the earth, whatever He was, we have been joined up to Him in one-ment.

The atonement is one-ment, meaning that the Lord has absolutely taken every vestige of human deformity, depravity, lack of comprehension, and inactivity of faith and has nailed it to the cross. It is forever on the cross. YOU died with Him on the cross. And if you will only believe you are dead with Him, you can believe you are dead indeed to sin and alive to righteousness.

The atonement—the one-ment principle, the working out of this wonderful regenerative power of God—moves us to say, "I am complete in His oneness." There is not one vestige of human weakness. If I dare believe it, I am so in order with God's Son that He makes me perfect! I am at one with Him, with no sin, no blemish, no failure. It is absolutely a perfect atonement, until there isn't a vestige of weakness left.

Dare you believe it? It may not be easy for you to, but I want to make it easy. Faith is the substance of things hoped for. Everything the Word of God speaks to you, faith lends its help. Faith stirs you. Faith says to you, "If you believe, it is now. If you dare believe now, oneness, purity, power, eternal fact are working through you."

Oneness—all are one in Christ, perfectly covered, hidden, "lost" in God's Son. He has made us whole through the blood. We have oneness, purity, divine association.

> *Wherefore, as by one man sin entered into the world, and death by sin; and so death passed upon all men, for that all have sinned:*
>
> *(For until the law sin was in the world: but sin is not imputed when there is no law.*

Nevertheless death reigned from Adam to Moses, even over them that had not sinned after the similitude of Adam's transgression, who is the figure of him that was to come.

But not as the offence, so also is the free gift. For if through the offence of one many be dead, much more the grace of God, and the gift by grace, which is by one man, Jesus Christ, hath abounded unto many.)

Romans 5:12-15

Through one man's disobedience, through one man's sin, death came and reigned. Now here is Another, a New Man. Adam was the first; Christ, the second. One was earthly; the other, heavenly. As sin reigned and as death reigned by one, so now the New Man, the Christ-man, shall make us awake to righteousness, to peace, to an abounding walk with God. Just as death had its power, through a New Man life has its power and victory. Through a New Man, we have come into a new divine order, *abounding*.

Abounding in Christ

It is probably difficult for you to claim it. "Abounding! I cannot understand it, Wigglesworth" you say.

No, brother, and you never will. The thought is a thousand times bigger than your mind. But *Christ's mind*, replanted in your natural order, will give you a vision so that you may see what you cannot understand. What you will never understand on your own, God thoroughly understands and abounds to you in blessed revelation. He says, *"Only believe, and it shall be abounding to you."*

God shall make it rich to you!

You know how sin was abounding, how we were held, how we were defeated, how we groaned and travailed. Has sin abounded? Yes, but there is now grace, life, and ministry abounding unto us.

Brother, sister, take a leap, that you may never know what defeat is anymore!

This is a real divine healing chapter, a real ascension chapter, a real power-of-resurrection chapter. It looses you from your limitations and brings an "unlimitation." It takes away the former, limited place you were in and brings you into a place of coveted grace. It takes your weaknesses and sins and bounds to you with atonement. It covers you with atonement. And it reveals to you all that Adam ever had which *bound* you and all that Christ ever had or will have which *abounds* toward you to liberate you from all that is human and to bring you into all that is divine, separating you forever.

This is the glorious liberty of the Gospel of Christ. This is abounding measure!

> *And not as it was by one that sinned, so is the gift: for the judgment was by one to condemnation, but the free gift is of many offences unto justification.*
>
> Romans 5:16

We have been condemned and lost before. How human nature destroys! We all know sin had its reign; but there is a justification, a mighty power of justifying, for those under its reign. God, working in the lower order with His mighty higher order, touches human weaknesses with His touch of finite, infinite, glorious resurrection power. *He transforms man!*

For if by one man's offence death reigned by one; much more they which receive abundance of grace and of the gift of righteousness shall reign in life by one, Jesus Christ.

Romans 5:17

Oh, how rich we are! There was a death-life, but it has been supplanted by a righteous life. You were in death, a death-life, but now you have a righteous life over death, over weaknesses.

How much have you received? Romans 5:17 says, *"...much more they which receive abundance of grace...."* You have received ABUNDANCE of grace. What does that mean? Your grace ran out years ago. My grace spun out years ago, but I realized and got to know by the revelation of the Spirit that His grace would take the place of my grace. His power in the grace would cover me where I could not cover myself. He would stand beside me when I was sure to go down. He would stretch out His hand in love and mercy toward me. He would never fail to be there every time I was sure to fail. That is abundance of grace. That is grace abounding.

Oh, the boundless mercy of the love of God to us! We were in sin, but *"...where sin abounded, grace did much more abound"* (Romans 5:20).

I hope you are getting this. I hope you thriving in it and triumphing in it. I hope you are coming to the place of seeing you are victor in it.

Mountain or Molehill?

A large number of people fail to come into access to God's gift because the knowledge of their own imperfection makes them fearful of God. Oh, the devil has a tremendous trap set all the time: He is trying to catch poor people who have made a little slip, or haven't said just the right thing. They have done nothing especially wrong, but the devil tries to make it seem like a mountain, when it is not more than molehill.

I go into this slowly, lest you miss it. The Word is line upon line and precept upon precept. It gives a lot of truth about being saved, about having the peace of God, and about being free in Christ.

But I find that Satan "dethrones" some of the loveliest people by catching them at a time when they are unaware. I find them all the time—poor souls!—deceived by the power of Satan. They need to hear this word: *When Satan is his nearest, God is NEARER, with an abounding measure of His grace.*

When you feel almost as though you would be defeated, God has a banner waving over you to cover you at that moment. He abounds toward you and covers you with His grace. He covers you with His righteousness, which is the very nature, the very life, of the Son of God.

Beloved, where you fail in your righteousness, Jesus Christ has for you a gift of righteousness, a super-planting of your righteousness, a taking away of your filthy garment and a clothing of you with a new garment. He has power to take away even thy tongue of evil and thy thoughts of evil. God's Son is so gracious toward us! His grace is abounding toward us much more.

God wants to supplant you with His righteousness, the righteousness of the Son of God. It has no adulteration or judgment in it. It is full of mercy and entreaty, for it is the righteousness of the law of God's Spirit. Dare you come into it? Dare, for there is a reigning position for you in the life God gives you.

Now, it is impossible for this life to remain in the body. When you are intoxicated with the Spirit, the Spirit-life flows through the avenues of your mind and the keen perception of the heart with deep throbbings. You are filled with the passion of the grace of God until you are filled with illumination by the power of the new wine (the wine of the kingdom: the Holy Ghost). Your whole body becomes intoxicated.

This is Rapture. This will have to leave the body. There is no natural body that is able to stand such a process as this! The life will have to leave; however, the body will be a preserver to it until the sons of God are made marvelously manifest.

You are a son of God, filled with His life. Sonship is a position of rightful heirship. Sons have a right to the first claiming of the will. As an heir of God and joint-heir with Christ (Romans 8:17), you have an inheritance to claim.

Liberality of Grace

I would like you to realize that redemption is perfect for getting rid of all your judgment of yourself. Start believing that God has a righteous judgment for you. Get away from all the powers of the devil; receive liberality of grace, which is much more abounding toward you. Grace abounding and righteousness abounding are liberty for the soul and transformation of the mind. They can lift you out of all your earthly place, into God's power and authority.

This holy new life, this presentation of the Son of God in your human body, this life in you, is so after the order of God, it is not ashamed in any way to say that you are coming into coequality with the Father, with the Son, and with the Holy Ghost.

God has been showing me that Jesus meant us when He said, "I will give *you* power to remit sin. Anybody's sin you remit will be remitted. And I will also give you power to do the opposite, to retain sin" (John 20:23, paraphrased).

The power of this verse was manifested in the days of the first apostles. We see it in Acts 13, when Elymas the sorcerer stood in the way of the power of the Holy Ghost. Filled with the Holy Ghost, Paul, an apostle of Jesus Christ, said to him, *"...thou child of the devil, thou enemy of all righteousness,... thou shalt be blind, not seeing the sun for a season..."* (Acts 13:10,11) Immediately, a mist and a darkness fell on him and he could not see.

In another instance, a man in the church was living in fornication. The apostle cast him over to Satan for the destruction of the flesh. Then a few months after they saw that Satan had done such havoc with his body and that this power of evil would take him to the grave, they took him out of the power of Satan and placed him back in the church.

We have to see that God, in the divine order, is bringing us into like-mindedness of faith. I speak this to you because I know the Holy Ghost is bringing the Church through. She has passed through many dark days of misunderstanding, but God is showing us that we have power to defeat the powers of the enemy. We have power to reign in this life by Another!

God has mightily justified us with grace abounding, filled us with the Holy Ghost, and given us the hope of the glory. When we were helpless, Jesus Christ came and took our place. And seeing that through Adam we all received evil things, Jesus gave a new impetus so grace could be where sin was and righteousness could be where there was no righteousness. He wants us to move from grace to grace, travailing in the Spirit till *the whole man* is longing for redemption.

Bless God! It is not far off; it is very near, at the door. Ah, there will be a shout some day! It will not be long before He shall be here!

> *Therefore as by the offence of one judgment came upon all men to condemnation; even so by the righteousness of one the free gift came upon all men unto justification of life.*
>
> *For as by one man's disobedience many were made sinners, so by the obedience of one shall many be made righteous.*
>
> *Moreover the law entered, that the offence might abound. But where sin abounded, grace did much more abound:*
>
> *That as sin hath reigned unto death, even so might grace reign through righteousness unto eternal life by Jesus Christ our Lord.*
>
> Romans 5:18-21

Eternal life is resurrection. Eternal life is with the Father and with the Son. Eternal life has come into us; and as the Father is, so are we. As the Son is, so are we. And the glory itself will not be able to contain His position without the glory of the earth coming to the glory which is in heaven.

This life eternal is manifested in mortal bodies. The life of Christ shall be so manifested in our mortal bodies that everything shall be dead indeed unto sin and alive unto God by the Spirit.

We are ready for it. We are gloriously ready! Oh, hallelujah!

A Holy Magnet

The life, the redemption, the glorious life in the Spirit—have you got it? Have you entered into it? Is it a reality to you? Do you know that it would not be possible for Him to move at all in the glory without *your* moving that way? It would be impossible for the Lord in His life to come without taking you.

One day I saw a great big magnet let down amongst iron. It picked up loads of iron and carried them away. That is a natural order, but ours is a spiritual order of a holy Magnet. That which is in thee is holy; that which is in thee is pure.

And when the Lord of righteousness shall appear, who is our life, then that which is holy, which is His nature, which is His life, shall go—and we shall be forever with the Lord!

You have not gone yet, *but you are sure to go.*

Seeing we are here, comforting one another, building up one another in the most holy faith, pray, *"Lord, let it please Thee for us to remain. But please, Father, let us be more holy here. Let us be more pure. Please, Father, let this life of thy Son eat up all mortality till there is nothing left but that which is to be changed in a moment; in the twinkling of an eye."*

Do not let one thought, one act, one thing in any way interfere with more Rapture. Ask God for every moment to be a moment of purifying, a moment of Rapture-seeking, a moment of a new order of the Spirit in your body. Let God take you into the fullness of redemption in a wonderful way.

Covet to be more holy.

Covet to be more separate .

Covet God.

Covet gifts.

Covet the graces.

Covet the beatitudes.

Covet earnestly.

May God show us that divine order so that love shall eat us up. It will be no sacrifice, but love eating our very nature until we love and love—until the whole Church is love.

Jesus said, "A new commandment I give you, that you should love one another" (John 13:34, paraphrased).

Pray, *"Oh, breathe this holy, intense love in our bosom today. Love! Love! Love! Let it please Thee, Lord, for this bond of union, this holy covenant with Thee, to be so strong, no man shall be able to separate us from this love of God in Christ Jesus. And whom the Lord hath joined together, let no power in the world put asunder. May love, love, LOVE take us on to the summit of the perfection: 'God so loved.'"*

(This sermon was preached on August 19, 1927.)

Chapter 7

Temptation Endured

Let the Spirit cover you today, that you may be intensely in earnest about the deep things of God.

You should be so much in the order of the Spirit that you know that your will, your mind, and your heart may be centered in God to such a point that He lifts you into the pavillion of splendor where you hear His voice. He lifts you to the place where the breath of the Almighty can send you to pray and send you to preach, with the Spirit of the Lord being upon you.

You are at the banquet of multiplication. It is a banquet of no separation. It is a banquet where you have to increase with all increasing, where God has for you riches beyond all things—not fleshly or carnal things, but spiritual manifestations (gifts, fruit of the Spirit, beautiful beautitudes)—with the blessings of God always being upon you.

Are you ready for this glorious place
Where you are dismissed, and God takes place,
To send you on your eternal race
To win thousands of people, that they may enter
into eternal grace?

For our study today the Lord has led me to select the first chapter of James. It has a marvelous subject in it. It is the Master's subject.

Tongues Interpretation

The Spirit moveth and changes His operation, bringing the soul into the place of hunger and desire, till the whole of the being cries out for the living God. Truly, the creature must be delivered from this present evil thing. So God is operating through us by these meetings and letting us know that all flesh is grass. But He also is bringing the Spirit of revelation, that we may know that this inheritance we are having is to endure forever and ever. For we belong to the new creation of God, clothed upon with the Spirit, made like unto Him.

Our whole hearts now are bringing forth that which God has established, and it out of the fullness of the truth of the hidden heart that God flows forth His glory, His power, His might, and His revelation in association. He makes us one and says, "Ye are Mine."

Victorious In Battle

James, a servant of God and of the lord Jesus Christ, to the twelve tribes which are scattered abroad, greeting. My brethren, count it all joy when ye fall into divers temptations.

James 1:1, 2

No person is ever able to talk about the victory over temptation unless he has gone through it. All victories are won in battles.

There are tens of thousands of people in the old land, and also in America and other parts of the world, who are wearing badges [medals] to show they have been in the battle. And they rejoice in it. They would be ashamed to wear a badge if they had not been in the battle. It is the battle that causes them to wear the badge.

It is those people who have been in the fight who tell about the victories. It is only James and Peter and Paul—those who were in the front line of the battle—who tell you we have to rejoice in the trial because there is wonderful blessing coming out of the trial: It is in the trial that we are made perfect.

Tribulation, Patience, Experience

You want an experience, do you? I will read you something that will give you an experience. I know nothing like it.

> *Therefore being justified by faith, we have peace with God through our lord Jesus Christ:*
>
> *By whom also we have access by faith into this grace wherein we stand, and rejoice in hope of the glory of God.*
>
> *And not only so, but we glory in tribulations also: knowing that tribulation worketh patience;*
>
> *And patience, experience....*
>
> Romans 5:1-4

And out of the experience, we tell what God is doing.

Do you want to have a big victory story to tell? Well, here it is. Just count it all joy in the midst of temptations (James 1:2)!

When the trial is severe—when you think that no one is tried as much as you—when the trial is so hard you cannot sleep and you do not know what to do—count it all joy. God has something divine in it.

You are in a good place when you do not know what to do. Your story of victory is forming.

After Abraham was tried, then he could offer Isaac—but not before he was tried. God put him through all kinds of tests. For twenty-five years, he was tested. He is called "the father of the faithful" because he did not give in to temptation. We have blessings today because one man dared to believe God without a move from Him for twenty-five years.

"Lord, You Have Done It!"

A woman came up to me in a meeting one day and said, "I have come for you to heal me. Can you see this big goiter?"

"I can hardly see anything else," I said.

She had told her father and mother and the family before she came that she believed she was going to be healed, because Wigglesworth was going to pray for her.

As soon as she was prayed for, we had a testimony meeting. Her testimony was wonderful.

"Oh" she said, "I thank God, because He has perfectly healed me!"

She went home, and they were all glad to hear what she said.

"When I was prayed for, I was perfectly healed!" she exultantly exclaimed.

For twelve months, she went all up and down among the assemblies, telling how God had healed her.

Twelve months later, I was in the same place. She came, filled with joy. When she walked in, the people said, "Oh, look how big that goiter is!" They were all looking on. By and by, we had a testimony meeting.

"Oh" she said, "twelve months ago, I was prayed for here and I was marvelously healed. I have had twelve months of the most wonderful time on the earth, because God so wonderfully healed me."

She went home. When she got home, she said to her mother, "Oh, if you had been there and seen the people! How they were moved when they heard me tell how God healed me!"

"Look!" the mother said, "You don't seem to know, but the people are believing there is something wrong with your mind, and they believe all the family is touched with it. You are bringing disgrace upon all the family. We are disgusted with you. It is shameful. The whole thing is rolled onto us because you are touched in your mind. Why don't you go look in the glass, and you will see the thing has not moved at all."

She went to her room. She said, "Lord, I do not want to look in the glass. I believe You have healed me. You have done it, but let all the people know that You have done it. Let them all know You have done it, just the same as You have let me know You have done it."

The next morning, she came downstairs as perfect as anybody could be, and the family knew the Lord had done it!

Believe, and You'll See the Glory of God

Some people, because they are not healed in a moment, wonder what is up. Maybe you wonder that. God never breaks His promise. The trial of your faith is much more precious than gold.

God has you in the earth so He can try to bring out His character in you. He wants to destroy the power of the devil. He wants to move you inside so that in the face of difficulties and hardships *you will want to praise the Lord.*

"Count it all joy," James 1:2 says. You have to take a joyful leap today. You have to leap into the promises. You have to believe God never fails you. You have to believe it is impossible for God to break His Word, because He is from everlasting to everlasting.

> *Forever and ever, not for a day,*
> *He keepeth His promise forever;*
> *To all who believe, to all who obey,*
> *He keepeth His promise forever.*

There is no variableness with God; there is no shadow of turning (James 1:17). He is always the same. He never fails to manifest His divine glory. To Mary and Martha He said, *"... if thou wouldest believe, thou shouldest see the glory of God"* (John 11:40).

We must understand that there will be testing times, but they are only to make us more like the Master. He was tempted in all points, like as we are, yet without sin. He endured all things. He is our example.

Oh, that God would give us an earnest, intent position where flesh and blood have to yield! We would go forward. We would not be moved by our feelings.

The man who is prayed for today gets a blessing; but tomorrow, because he does not feel exactly as he ought to, he begins murmuring. What is he doing? He is changing the Word of God for his feelings.

What an awful disgrace it is for you to change the Word of God because of your feelings! Let God have His perfect work.

The phrase *"count it all joy"* does not mean "count a bit of it joy" but "count it ALL joy." It doesn't matter from what direction your trial comes: whether from the direction of your business, your home, or whatever—you are to count it all joy. Why? *"We know that all things work together for good to them that love God, to them who are called according to his purpose"* (Romans 8:28).

That is a great word. It indicates that you have a special position where God is "electrifying" the very position of you so that the devil will see there is a character about you. And he will have to say something about you, as he said about Job in Job 1.

"Satan, what is your opinion about Job?" the Lord asked. "Don't you think he is wonderful? Don't you think he is the most excellent of all the earth? Isn't he beautiful?"

"Yes, but You know You are keeping him," the devil said. (Praise the Lord! I am glad the devil has to tell the truth. And don't you know, God can keep *you*!)

"If You touch his body," the devil said, "he will curse You to your face."

"You do it. But you cannot touch his life," God said.

(The Scriptures say that Jesus was dead, but is alive again, and hath power over death and hell; at that, there is a big "AMEN!" [Revelation 1:18]. Jesus has power over the devil. The devil cannot take your life unless the Lord allows it.)

"Thou shalt not touch his life," God commanded.

(The devil thought he could do it, and you know the calamity he caused in Job's life. But Job said, "Naked came I into the world, and naked shall I go out. Blessed be the Name of the Lord!" [Job 1:21].)

Oh, it is lovely! The Lord can give us that same language Job had. It is not a language of the head. It is a divine language; it is of a *heart* acquaintance with God.

I want you to know that you can have a heart acquaintance. It is far better to speak out of the abundance of your *heart* than out of the abundance of your *head*. I learned a long time ago that nothing but libraries make swelled heads, and nothing but THE Library makes swelled hearts.

You are to have swelled hearts, because out of a heart that is full of the fragrance of the love of God issues forth the living life of the Lord.

Tongues Interpretation

It is the Spirit that giveth liberty. The prophet is nothing; but the Spirit brings us into attainment, where we sit at His feet, and seek with Him, and have communications of things divine. For now, we are not belonging to the earth; we are transformed by the renewing of our mind and set in heavenly places with Christ Jesus.

You must cease to be. That may be a difficult thing for you to do, but it is no trouble at all when you are in the hands of the Potter. It is only hard when you are kicking! You are all right when you are still, and He is forming you afresh. Let Him form you afresh today and make another vessel, so that you will stand the stress.

Be Perfect

But let patience have her perfect work, that ye may be
perfect and entire, wanting nothing.

James 1:4

Oh, is it possible to be perfect? Certainly, it is possible. Who is saying so? It is the breath of the Spirit. It is the hidden man of the heart of a man who has a heart like his brother's. The Holy Spirit is speaking through James, the Lord's brother. James speaks very much like his brother. Likely enough, we might expect when we read these wonderful words that we, too, have a kindred spirit with the Lord.

James had to learn patience. It was not an easy thing for him to understand how his brother could be the Son of God and be living in the same house with his brothers Judas, Josiah, and the others. He had to learn to be patient, to see how it all worked out.

There are many things in your life that you cannot understand. But be patient, for when the hand of God is upon a thing, it may grind very slowly, but it will form the finest thing possible, if you dare wait until the end of it.

Don't kick until you are through—and when you are dead enough, you will never kick at all. It is a death come to death, that we might be alive unto God. It is only by the deaths we die that we are able to be still.

The cross? I can despise the cross.

The shame? I can despise it,

The bitter language spoken 'round,

"If Thou be the Christ, come down!

And we will believe!"

He stood it.

They smote Him;

But He reviled not again.

Jesus is the picture of patience for us. He was patient, enduring the cross and despising the shame. Why? He knew that as He came to the uttermost end of the cross, He would save the Los Angeles people forever. He would save all men forever.

You cannot tell what God has in mind for you. As you are still, being pliable in the hands of God, He will work out a greater vessel, probably greater than you could ever imagine in all your life.

Don't Be Moved

"Let patience have her perfect work, that you might be...entire..." (James 1:4). "Entirety" means that you are not moved by anything, but rather are living only in the divine position of God. "Entirety" means that you are not moved, or changed, by what people say.

The mighty God instills something strong in you through divine acquaintance. The new life God gives you is not surface. It builds the character in purity, until the inward heart is filled with divine love and has nothing but the thoughts of God alone. *"...that ye may be perfect and entire, wanting nothing,"* James 1:4 says. Wanting NOTHING!

Some people came to me in New Zealand and said, "We would like to make you a Christmas present, if you can tell us what you would like."

"I haven't a want in the world," I said. "I cannot tell you what I'd like. I have no desire for anything; only God."

Another time, I was walking down the street with a millionaire. I was feeling wonderfully happy over the way the Lord was blessing in our meetings. As we walked together, I said, "Brother, I haven't a care in the world. I am as happy as a bird!"

"Oh, stop!" he said. "Say it again! Say it again!" and he stood still, waiting for me to repeat it .

"Brother, I haven't a care in the world. I am as happy as a bird!"

"Oh, I would give all my money," he said, "I would give everything I have, to have that!"

We can be wanting *nothing*. Hallelujah!

The Spirit of the Lord is moving us mightily to see that this all has to do with resurrection power. We were planted with Him. We have risen with Him. We are from above; we do not belong to what is beneath. We reign in life by Another; by the life of God's Son, manifest in this human body.

Ask God for Wisdom

If any of you lack wisdom, let him ask of God, that giveth to all men liberally, and upbraideth not; and it shall be given him.

But let him ask in faith, nothing wavering.. .

For let not that man think that he shall receive any thing of the Lord.

James 1:5-7

Many people come to me and ask if I will pray for them to have faith. I want to encourage them, but I cannot go away from God's Word. I cannot grant people faith.

But by the power of the Spirit, I *can* stimulate you until you dare to believe and rest on the authority of God's Word. The Spirit of the living God quickens you. *"...faith cometh by hearing, and hearing by the word of God"* (Romans 10:17), and this is a living Word of faith: *"If any of you lack wisdom, let him ask of God, that giveth to all men liberally..."* (James 1:5).

One thing you have never experienced is God judging you for the wisdom He gave you, or for the blessing He gave you. He makes it so that when you come to Him again, He gives again, never asking what you did with the last blessing. That is the way God gives: God *"...giveth...liberally, and upbraideth not..."* (James 1:5). Therefore, you have a chance today to come to Him for much more! Do you want wisdom? Ask of God.

Tongues Interpretation

It is not wisdom that you get from the earth; it is divine wisdom that brings a peaceful position. It ruleth with diligence, and it causes you to live in quietness. You know the difference between the wisdom which is from above and the wisdom which is from beneath.

And so the Spirit breathes through our brother to show you that you have to be so in the perfect will of God in asking for these things until one thing must be fulfilled in your heart. If you ask, you must believe, or God is only pleased when you believe.

You have to be in the order of asking. This is the order: *"But let him ask in faith, nothing wavering..."* (James 1:6).

I am satisfied that God, who is the builder of divine order, never brings confusion into His order.

It was only when things got out of order that God brought confusion. When the people who were building a tall tower asked for bricks, they were given straw. They were out of order. They were trying to get into heaven some other way, and they were thieves and robbers. So God turned their language and their whole plan to confusion. There is a way into the kingdom of heaven: It is only through the blood of the Lord Jesus Christ!

If you want divine order in your life—if you want wisdom—you have to come to God, believing.

I want to impress upon you the fact—and I am learning the truth of it more every day—that if you ask six times for anything, it shows you are an unbelieving person. If you really believe, you will ask God only once. And that is all you need to do, because He has abundance for your every need. But if you go right to Him and ask six times, instead of one, He knows very well you do not believe He'll give what you ask—so you do not get it. God does not honor unbelief; He honors faith.

If you would really get down to business about the baptism of the Holy Ghost, ask God definitely and *once* to fill you, and *believe* it, what would you do? You would begin to praise Him for it, because you know He has given it!

If you ask God once for healing, you will get it. But if you ask a thousand times a day, until you aren't even aware you are still asking, you will get nothing. If you would ask God for your healing now, and begin praising Him because He never breaks His Word and will heal you as the Word promises, you would go out perfect. *Only believe.*

God wants to promote you. He wants you to get away from your own thoughts and your own foolishness and get to a definite place where you believe that He is, and that He is a Rewarder of them that seek Him diligently.

Have you gotten to the place where you dare to believe God and count it all joy? Have you gotten to the place where you are going to murmur no more when you are in a trial? Are you going to be weeping, telling people about it, or are you going to say, "Thank You, Lord, for putting me on the top?"

Many people do not get checks sent to them because they didn't thank the donor for the last one. Many people get no blessing because they did not thank God for the last one. A thankful heart is a receiving heart. God wants to keep you in the place of constant believing with thanksgiving so you will receive.

> *Keep on believing Jesus is near,*
> *Keep on believing there's nothing to fear;*
> *Keep on believing—this is the way:*
> *Faith in the night, the same as the day.*

Endured Temptation Brings the Crown

Blessed is the man that endureth temptation: for when he is hied, he shall receive the crown of life, which the Lord hath promised to them that love him.

James 1:12

People do not know what they are getting when they are in a great place of temptation. Temptation endured brings the crown of life!

> *Let no man say when he is tempted, I am tempted of God: for God cannot be tempted with evil, neither tempteth he any man:*
>
> *But every man is tempted, when he is drawn away of his own lust, and enticed.*
>
> *Then when lust hath conceived, it bringeth forth sin: and sin, when it is finished, bringeth forth death.*
>
> *Do not err, my beloved brethren.*
>
> James 1:13-16

There is nothing outside of purity that is not sin. *All unbelief is sin.* God wants you to have a pure, active faith, so you will be living all the time in an advanced place of believing Him. You will be on the mountaintop, singing, when other people are crying.

I want to speak now about lust. I am not speaking about the menial things, about the carnal desires, abut adultery, fornication, and such things. I am speaking about anything that has turned you aside to some other thing instead of God. God has been offering you better things all the time, and you have missed it if you have been turning to something else.

Three blessings are available to us in life, but I notice that many people are satisfied with having only one. There is a blessing in *justification*, a blessing in *sanctification* and a blessing in *the baptism of the Holy Ghost*.

Salvation is a wonderful thing (we all know that). Sanctification is a process which take us on to a higher height with God. The fullness of the Spirit is a process, too, just as salvation and sanctification are.

Any number of people are satisfied with "good"—salvation. Other people are satisfied with "better"—a sanctified life; a life purified by God. Other people are satisfied with "best"—the fullness of God, with revelation from on high.

I am not satisfied with any of the three. I am only satisfied with "best" *with improvement.* I come to you, not with "good" but better"; not with "better" but "best"; not with "best" but "best" with improvement: *going on with God.*

If we are going on with God, we won't give in to lust, because we know that *".. .when lust hath conceived bringeth forth sin; and sin, when it is finished, bringeth forth death"* (James 1:15). When anything takes us from God, it means death in some way.

When Jesus told His disciples that the Son of Man would be put into the hands of sinners and crucified, Peter remonstrated with Him. But Jesus said, "Get thee behind me, Satan, for thou savourest not the things of heaven, but the things of the earth" (Matthew 16:23, paraphrased).

Anything that hinders me from going to death is of the devil; anything that hinders me from being separated unto God is of the devil; and anything which hinders me from being purified every day is carnal—and brings death!

I pray for you today, that there would be no lustful thing in you that would rob you of the glory. May God take you to the very summit of the blessing, where you can be increased day by day into all the fullness of God.

Another word I want to tell you is this: God has wrought out the whole, beautiful plan of our inheritance, and we are brought into His spiritual order through the Word.

> *Wherefore, my beloved brethren, let every man be swift to hear, slow to speak, slow to wrath:*
>
> *For the wrath of man worketh not the righteousness of God.*
>
> *Wherefore lay apart all filthiness and superfluity of naughtiness, and receive with meekness the engrafted word, which is able to save your souls.*
>
> James 1:19-21

Do not neglect the Word of God. Take time to think about the Word of God. It is the only place of safety.

(July 22, 1927)

Chapter 8

The Clothing of the Spirit for the World's Need

Only believe! *Only believe!* God will not fail you, beloved. It is IMPOSSIBLE for God to fail. Believe Him. Rest in Him, for God's rest is an undisturbed place where heaven bends to meet you. God will fulfill the promises made to you in His Word—believe it!

Now, the Bible is the most important book in the world, but some people haven't spent time in it. They need to press in before they can press *on*.

Oh, the glorious inheritance of holy joy and faith the Word says we have! The glorious baptism in the Holy Ghost it speaks of is a perfected place! We read that all things are become new in our lives because we are Christ's, and Christ is God's! As we press in to truths such as these in God's Word, we will be able to press on to live in God's "royal way."

The Royal Way

But ye shall receive power, after the Holy Ghost is come upon you: and ye shall be witnesses unto me both in Jerusalem, and in all Judaea, and in Samaria, and unto the uttermost part of the earth.

Acts 1:8

God means for us to be in this royal way: in the power of the Holy Ghost, being God's witnesses in the earth. It's the door He wants us to walk through. And when God opens a door, no man can shut it. Through John the Baptist, He made a royal way, and Jesus went in. Now He has left it for us, so He can bring forth greater works through us than those done when Jesus walked the earth. Jesus left His disciples with much, but much more is to be added to us until God receives us in that day.

When we receive power, we must stir ourselves up to the truth that we are responsible for the need around us. God will supply our need so that the needs of the needy may be met through *us*. What a great, indwelling force of power! If we don't slip into our privileges to meet needs, it is a tragedy.

No Standing Still

God, who ravishes us, brings forth new revelation within the heart. He causes us to be changed by the Spirit from vision to vision, grace to grace, and glory to glory.

There is no standing still for us. As Christ is, so are we in this world: the offspring of God, with impulse divine. We must get into line! We have the life of the Son of God in us to make the whole Body aflame with fire. We have what it takes to do it, for the Word says, "More ye have received, ye shall have *power*" (Acts 1:8, paraphrased).

God has given me a blessed ministry. He helps me stir others up. Our gathering in meetings must be for increase; we must use the power of God in us to win more souls into the kingdom of God. I am zealous for us to come into this divine plan. If we wait for such power, we have mistaken the position we have through the Spirit.

God Is Waiting—So ACT!

"If I could only *feel* the power," we say.

We have been too much on that line. God is waiting for us to *act*, to be like Jesus. Jesus had "perfect activity"; He lived in the realm of divine appointment with the Father's acts ever coming forth.

The pure in heart see God, and our God is a consuming fire. We must dare to press on until God comes forth through us in mighty power. May God give us faith, that the power may come down like a cloud!

When I was in Slovanger, Norway, God said, *Ask! I will give you every soul.*

It seemed too much to ask! The voice came again: Ask!

I dared to ask. The power of God swept through the meeting like a mighty wind! You want this where you live, so speak all the Word of this life. Press on until Jesus is glorified and multitudes are gathered in.

(England, 1925)

Smith and Mary Jane (Polly) Wigglesworth pose with their five children: Alice, Seth, Harold, Ernest, and George.

Four generations of the Wigglesworth family.

Smith Wigglesworth and his daughter, Alice Salter, a missionary to Africa who also greatly assisted her father in his ministry.

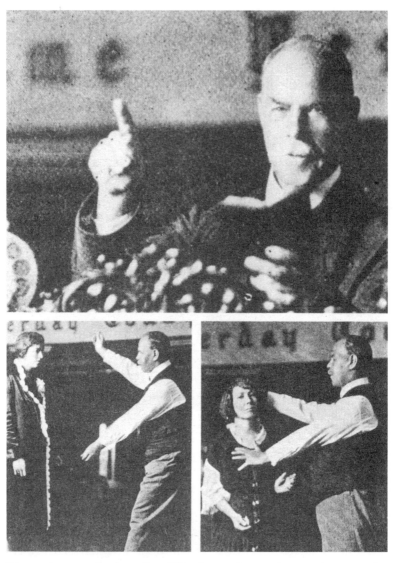

These photographs show Rev. Wigglesworth preaching and praying for the sick in 1927 in Aimee Semple McPherson's famous Angelus Temple, Los Angeles. He said he had a greater anointing to minister there than any place he had ever been.

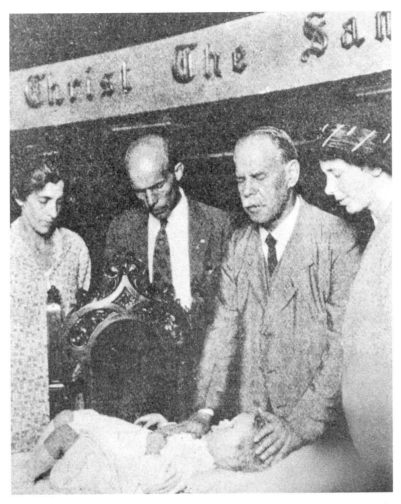

Rev. Wigglesworth prays for a sick child in 1927 at Aimee Semple Mcpherson's Angelus Temple, Los Angeles.

Smith Wigglesworth at age 67. (From the collection of Faith Campbell, daughter of pioneer Pentecostal editor Stanley Frodsham.)

The most widely published photograph of Smith Wigglesworth.

This handsome portrait shows the healing evangelist seated.

An informal photograph of Wigglesworth the world traveler in 1941. He went home to be with the Lord in 1947

On his trips to the United States, Smith Wigglesworth often spoke to students in Bible schools, such as this one.

Shortly before his death, Smith Wigglesworth expressed the desire that his custom-made container for anointing oil be given to the Rev. Myron Sackett, D.D.

In 1982 Paul Croft presented Smith Wigglesworth's New Testament to Dr. Buddy Harrison, founder and president of Faith Christian Fellowship International Church, Tulsa. These items were photographed through the courtesy of Mrs. May Sackett and Dr. Harrison. *Photos by Paul Meerholz.*

Chapter 9

Praying for the Sick

We need to be very close to God so that every day can bring us closer to our "goal" to glory, which has many wonderful things in it. I look forward to receiving the terrestrial body, which will be beautiful in every way (1 Corinthians 15:40). It will take in *all* the glories and *all* the expression of heaven.

I want to provoke you to this holy, inward interest so that you, too, may have a share in it. I look forward to the fulfillment of the Word of God, which says that He will bring many sons into glory (Hebrews 2:10).

I long to make you hungry to be sons of God; hungry to be worthy of redemption. I want to make you unable to rest unless you are feeling you are reaching the prize of the mark of your high calling in Christ Jesus (Philippians 3:14).

Be Ready

You must come into a place where you can earnestly contend for the faith delivered unto you. It is then that there will be no lack in your life. You will be *filled* with the grace of the Spirit and moved by almightiness. You will be ready for the many things God has for us in this day. And we *must* be ready. That is why I try to provoke you to holiness, intensity of desire, and an inward cry after God.

Pray, *"O Lord help me! Help me, that I may earnestly contend for the faith, leaving all things behind me and pressing forward to the prize."*

Are you ready today? Are you anxious today? Are you willing today? Oh, it was wonderful that some were willing in the day of their visitation from God! It is lovely to be in a place such as they were, where we can say, *"Mine eyes have seen thy salvation"* (Luke 2:30).

Are you ready? What for? To be so moved by the power of God that this day shall be eclipsed on every line, because of God taking me on with Him.

Are you ready? What for? To so lose yourself in God today that you will not claim your earthly rights, but claim the rights of your heavenly Father.

Are you ready? What for? To be able to so cry aloud that the Lord Himself will be the only one who can satisfy the desire of your heart.

Fresh Bread From God

If you are going on with God, you cannot be fed with natural bread. The people who are going on with God have to have the spiritual bread; bread that came down from heaven (John 6:51). This bread is fresh every day. It is very special, because it perfectly meets the need of every heart.

The disciples knew of this bread. They were listening to Jesus as He spoke marvelous words about it. They knew that there was a freshness about it, and they said, "Give us this bread!"

This is the bread that came down from heaven: the Son of God, who gave His life for the world (John 6:50,51). He is the bread of *life* (John 6:48). He has so wonderfully overcome the power of Satan, all the powers of disease, all the powers of sin, until there is a perfect place in Him where we may have abundant life. We may be free from all sin, sickness, disease, and death! It is one of the greatest positions that God has for us.

If I were to select a message to meet your need, you would find it in Romans 8:

> *There is therfore now no condemnation to them which are in Christ Jesus, who walk not after the flesh, but after the Spirit.*
>
> *For the law of the Spirit of life in Christ Jesus hath made me free from the law of sin and death.*
>
> Romans 8:1, 2

Reigning on the Rock

You see my message to you is as clear, definite, and personal as it could be: *In Christ Jesus you are free from the law of sin and death and all condemnation!*

As we enter into the knowledge of this divine plan, you will find that sin is dethroned, disease cannot hold its seat, death has lost its sting, and victory is in Christ Jesus.

You are reigning in life by Christ Jesus! To reign in life means that you are over every human weakness in every area of life. To reign means that you are standing on the Rock, and everything is under your feet.

Jesus has made a place of victory for all of us, that we may reign as a king over our bodies in every way and over all thoughts of evil. (Remember, thoughts of evil are from Satan. Evil thoughts come from within, so you must be wholly cleansed inwardly.)

If you are sick, you can experience healing.

Is any among you afflicted? let him pray....

James 5:13

Whenever I go to homes to pray for the sick, I turn to this, because this Scripture belongs to the Church. Are any in the Church sick? They should call for the elders. The elders will pray over them in the Name of the Lord and anoint the sick ones with oil—and they will be healed. (See James 5:14,15.)

I have had many revelations along the line of sicknesses, but I realize I must speak to you in as simple a form as possible. This is the keynote of many marvelous words God has been revealing to me: "Are you afflicted? Pray" (James 5:13, paraphrased). There must be prayer.

Healing Through Anointed Handkerchiefs

We were having some meetings in Belfast, Ireland, and the Lord was very graciously blessing us. The crowds were gathering. Many needy cases were helped. God was touching souls. A great many people began inviting us to pray for the sick in their homes.

This is a very difficult thing to do, but God has made a plan for us to take care of such emergencies. Consider Sister Aimee Semple

McPherson.[3] We know as well as anything that she *cannot* reach the hundreds which are longing for her to minister personally to them. She will never reach them; she cannot reach them. She has neither the strength nor the power to run from place to place.

Paul was in the same predicament at Ephesus. The cry for help was coming from many places. Paul knew there must be something that could reach this kind of need. He had a revelation. Paul was great on revelation, and then he wrote it down. We find that word in Acts 19.

> *And God wrought special miracles by the hands of Paul:*
>
> *So that from his body were brought unto the sick handkerchiefs or aprons, and the diseases departed from them, and the evil spirits went out of them.*
>
> Acts 19:11, 12

Paul would pray over a handkerchief or apron and then send it to a suffering one. The person's disease would be healed!

To create a great blessing in you, I want to tell you a story about praying over handkerchiefs for those we personally cannot reach. In Liverpool, a woman came to me and said, "I would like you to pray for my husband. He comes home drunk every night."

"Why, my dear sister" I said, "God has made a way for that."

"What way is it?" she asked.

"If you have a handkerchief," I said, "I will pray over it."

---

3   Aimee Semple McPherson, a minister of the Gospel who founded the Foursquare denomination and built Angelus Temple in Los Angeles

She opened her bag and brought out a handkerchief. I laid my hands upon it, prayed in the Name of Jesus, and gave it back to her. "What shall I do with it?" she asked.

"Place it upon his pillow," I answered.

"But he will be drunk."

"It makes no difference; he will have his drunken head on the promise of God."

She took the handkerchief and placed it on the pillow. He came home drunk. He knew nothing about the handkerchief. He slept all night and awoke in the morning, for all he knew, just as he was before.

Of course, it was his natural desire to call at the first saloon for some beer. He got the beer and began to take it. Instantly, he was convinced there was poison in the beer. He said to the bartender, "What have you done with that beer?"

"I have done nothing with it," the man answered.

"I know you have. I wouldn't take it for the world."

He went to another place, called for a glass of beer again, put it more cautiously to his lips, and was more convinced than ever there was poison in it. He said to the man, "Why has all Liverpool agreed to poison me?"

He worked all the morning and then went to a saloon at noon, as usual, to get his beer for lunch. This time he was convinced that Liverpool had agreed to poison him. He talked so much about it, he was asked to leave the place.

At night, he was determined not to go home without the beer. This time he was so enraged at the people who served him the beer, convinced it contained poison, that they had to throw him out of that place.

He went home without a drink, and his wife said, "My dear, why are you home so early?"

"You ought to pray for me," he said.

"Oh, I am."

"But you don't know, all Liverpool has agreed to poison me."

As he told her the story, she said, "Can't you see how the grace of God has covered you today? Can't you see how you have been delivered?"

He was awakened to consciousness that night and was blessedly saved. And—I am a witness—he became a wonderful worker for God.

It Is the Book

A woman sent a handkerchief to me to pray over. She had cancer and was at the point of death. I returned the handkerchief, and those close to her placed it on her. Instantly, God sent a new life through her. She was healed that day.

I could go on and on like this, but there is no need. Look—it is the Book. It is not Wigglesworth; it is the Book. Praying over handkerchiefs is God's remedy in the Book for people like me, Mrs. McPerson, and others of us who cannot reach the people to bring healing to them.

When God moves, He will move you biblically. When you move *biblically*, you will move savingly, healingly, cleansingly, and heavenly.

In our meetings in Norway and Sweden, five hundred handkerchiefs were brought for prayer at one meeting. In Ceylon, one thousand were brought at one meeting!

"Is Anyone Sick?"

"Is there anyone sick? Is there anyone sick in this placer"—this is what I ask when I go into a room with sick people in it. Why? I will tell you a story which will explain.

I am interested in and help support missionaries all over the world. My own daughter is a missionary in Africa. I love missionary work. We had a missionary in China who, one way or another, got rheumatism.

I have no definition for rheumatism except "devil possessed." Rheumatism, cancers, tumors, lumbago, neuralgia—to all these things I give only one name: "the power of the devil working in humanity." When I see sickness, I see demon-working power.

But all these things can be removed by the power of God!

When Jesus went into Peter's mother-in-law's house, what did He do when He found out she was sick? Did He cover her up with a blanket and put a hot water bottle to her feet? If He didn't, why didn't He? Because He knew it was *demons* that had all the heat of hell in them. He did the right thing; He rebuked the fever, and it left.

We, too, ought to do the right thing with diseases. We should rebuke them in the Name of Jesus!

The missionary with rheumatism came home to Belfast from China, enraged against the work of God, enraged against God, enraged against everything. She was absolutely outside the plan of God.

While in Belfast, God allowed this missionary to fall down the steps and dislocate her backbone. She had to be lifted up and carried to her bed. God allowed it.

Be careful about falling out with God because of something wrong with your body. Get right with God, and stay right with Him.

She asked me to come visit her. When I walked into her room, I looked at her and said, "Is there anyone sick in this room?"

No response.

"Is there anyone sick in the room?"

No response again.

"Well," I said, "we will wait until someone moves."

By and by, she said, "Yes, I am sick."

"We have found you out then. You are in the room. Now, the Word of God says that when you are sick, you are to pray. When you pray," I said, "I will anoint you and I will pray for you—*but not before.*"

It took her almost a quarter of an hour to yield, because the devil had such possession of her. But she finally yielded, thank God. Then she cried and cried, and her body, by the power of God, was shaken loose from the disease. She was made free when she repented, but not before.

What would happen if everybody in this meeting would repent today? Talk about blessings! The glory would fall so much, the people wouldn't be able to get out of the place. We need to see that God wants us to be blessed; but, first of all, He wants us to be *ready* for the blessing by being right with Him.

Look to God

I want to take you to another word about this.

Brethren, if any of you do err from the truth, and one convert him;

Let him know, that he which converteth the sinner from the error of his way shall save a soul from death, and shall hide a multitude of sins.

James 5:19, 20

One thing God is showing me, which causes me to deal very faithfully with sick people, is this: If the first remedy you had taken from the doctor's bottle had healed you, you would not be here at this meeting, wanting prayer from me. You are only giving God the next chance.

If we would be as faithful to God as we have been to doctors, we would all be healed. But we have been unfaithful, and there is need of repentance.

Some people go back to medicine after they have been healed. Verse 19 shows what the Bible says about that. People preach on this verse and turn it into a salvation message. But it has nothing to do with salvation; it is a *healing* message, and it is full of life. It says, *"Brethren, if any of you do err from the truth...."*

What is "erring from the truth"? Erring is when you use remedies after God has healed you. After you have tried all you can get of all kinds of remedies, but they don't help you, then you are in a predicament.

Someone comes along and turns you "from the error of your way"; he must save you from your sin of turning from God to seek other means. If he does, he is saving you from death.

God is so merciful after all our erring! What I am doing is turning you from the error of your ways to get back to the God of mercy. Look to God! Only believe that His atoning blood is *sufficient*, and you may be healed from every weakness!

The God who told Moses to make a pole and put a brazen serpent upon it so that whoever looked at it could be healed now says, "The brazen serpent is not on the pole. Jesus is not on the cross. So now BELIEVE. You shall be healed, if you believe."

You cannot look to the cross. You cannot look to the serpent. But you *can* believe in the living God. And if you believe, you can be healed. God means for you to look to Him today; He means for you to be helped today!

Complete vs. Partial Healing

I want everyone to know that Wigglesworth does not believe in partial healing.

Then what does Wigglesworth believe? I believe in *complete healing*. Even if it is not manifested, it is there all the same. It is indolent because of inactive faith, but it is there. God has given it.

How do I know this is true? Mark 16:18 states, "*...they shall lay hands on the sick, and they shall recover.*" Whose Word is that? It is God's Word! I have faith in that today. Hallelujah! Even repeating the Word gives me more faith!

Tongues Interpretation

Why dost thou doubt when God, even the Lord, hath come to cast the devil out, that you may know you are free from all things by the blood of Jesus?

We are in a great place; the Lord is in the midst of us. You are to go away *free* today.

Healed With His Stripes

I like the thought that *"Himself took our infirmities, and bare our sicknesses"* (Matthew 8:17). It is a powerful thought!

One day I was standing at the bottom of Shanklin Road, Belfast, Ireland, with a piece of paper in my hand, looking at the addresses of where I had to go. A man came over and said to me, "Are you visiting the sick?"

"Yes," I said.

"Go there," he said, pointing to a nearby house.

I knocked at the door, but there was no reply. I knocked again, and then a voice inside said, "Come in!"

I opened the door and walked in. A young man pointed for me to go up the stairway. When I got up onto the landing, I saw a wide-open door. I walked right into the doorway and found a woman sitting up on the bed. As soon as I looked at her, I knew she couldn't speak to me, so I began to pray. She was moving backwards and forwards, gasping for breath. I knew she was beyond answering me.

When I prayed, the Lord distinctly said to me, *Read Isaiah 53.*

I opened the Book and began to read from the beginning, *"Who hath believed our report? and to whom is the arm of the Lord revealed? For he shall grow up before him as a tender plant, and as a root out of a dry ground."*

When I got to the fifth verse—*"He was wounded for our transgressions, he was bruised or our iniquities: the chastisement of our peace was upon him; and with his stripes we are healed"*—the woman shouted, "I am healed!"

"Oh, woman," I said, "tell me."

"Three weeks ago, I was cleaning the house," she said. "In moving some furniture, I strained my heart. It moved out of its place. The doctors examined me and said that I would die with suffocation—and, truly, it often has been as though I would die with suffocation.

"But in the middle of the night last night, I saw you come into the room. When you saw me, you knew I could not speak, so you began to pray. Then you opened to Isaiah 53 and read until you came to the fifth verse. And when you read the fifth verse, I was completely healed. That was a vision; now it is a *fact*!"

So I know the Word of God is still true!

Tongues Interpretation

Stretch out thy hand, for the Lord thy God is so nigh unto thee! He shall take thee and so place thee in His pavilion of splendor that, if thou wilt not go out any more, but remain stationary in the will of God, He shall grant thee the desire of thy heart.

Now, that is a Word from the Lord. You will never get anything more distinctly than that from the Lord. Yes, people miss the greatest plan of healing because of moving from one thing to another. Become stationary.

God wants you to take the Word; claim the Word; believe the Word. That is the perfect way of healing. Turn neither to the right hand nor the left, but BELIEVE GOD!

God's Touch Heals

I believe we ought to have people in this meeting loosed from their infirmities without being touched. More and more, I see that the day of visitation of the Lord is upon us. The presence of the Lord is here to heal. We should have people healed under the unction of the Spirit in these meetings while I am speaking.

I have been preaching along these lines of faith so that you may definitely claim your healing. I believe if you listen to the Lord, and if you are moved to believe (if you stand up while I pray), you will find that healing virtue will loose you.

Tongues Interpretation

In the depths, God has come and moves in the very inner working of the heart, till the Spirit of the Lord becomes the perfect choice. He brings forth that which shall resound to His glory forever. The Lord is in the midst of it, and those that are bound are made free from captivity.

God wants you to have a living faith NOW, to get a vital touch NOW that shakes the foundation of all weakness. When you were saved, you were saved the MOMENT you believed. And you will be healed the MOMENT you believe, too.

I pray, *"Father, into thy gracious care I take these people and present them to Thee. Keep them from falling; keep them from the error of the ways of the wicked; deliver them from all evil. Let thy mercy be with them in their homes, in their bodies, in EVERY way."*

(July 6, 1927)

Chapter 10

Overcoming

I think it will please God if I read you the fifth chapter of the First Epistle of John.

> *Whosoever believeth that Jesus is the Christ is born of God: and every one that loveth him that begat loveth him also that is begotten of him.*
>
> *By this we know that we love the children of God, when we love God, and keep his commandments. For this is the love of God, that we keep his commandments: and his commandments are not grievous.*
>
> *For whatsoever is born of God overcometh the world: and this is the victory that overcometh the world, even our faith.*
>
> *Who is he that overcometh the world, but he that believeth that Jesus is the Son of God?*
>
> 1 John 5:1-5

This is one of those wonderful, divine truths of God which brings to the life heart-affection, which verifies in every condition of life that it is of God. This is one of those essential truths which gives us a clear discernment of our position in Christ.

God wants all of us to be built up in truth, righteousness, and the life of God, so every person we come in contact with may know of a truth that we are of God; and we who are of God can assure our hearts before Him and have perfect confidence.

There is something more in the believer than words. Words are of little effect unless they have a personal manifestation of God. We must not look at the Word as only a written Word. The Word is a live fact, working in the human body living truths—changing it, moving it—until the person is a living fact of God's inheritance; until He is in the body, reigning in the world over the world. Thus, in conversation or activity, the person is a production of God. It is truly a human plan first, but it is covered with God's inheritance!

Born of God

I want to come to the Word itself and, by the grace of God, bring us into a place where it would be impossible, whatever happens, to move us from our plan. Let us look at the first verse: *"Whosoever believeth that Jesus is the Christ is born of God: and every one that loveth him that begat loveth him also that is begotten of him"* (1 John 5:1).

There are hundreds of religions, so called, crowded everywhere. But look! All these differences of opinions wither away.

There is to be a *perfect* oneness and *divine* union, and it will surely have to come to pass. You ask, "How is it possible?"

What I'm going to say is truth; it is the Word of God; it is God Himself portrayed in the Word. We see God in the Word. God can manifest Himself through that Word until we become a living factor of that truth, because God is light, and in Him is no darkness. God is life. God is revelation. God is manifestation. And God is operation.

God wants to bring us into a place where we truly have the clearest revelation of where we stand.

"Whosoever believeth that Jesus is the Christ is born of God" (1 John 5:1). What is the outcome of being born of God? God's life, truth, walk, communion, fellowship, oneness, and like-mindedness become ours. All that pertains to holiness, righteousness, and truth comes forth out of this New Birth unto righteousness. And in it, through it, and by it we have a perfect regenerated position, just as we have come into light through this.

Again, it is an impartation of love—an expression of Himself—for God is love. The first breathing or revelation of light of the new creation within the soul is so pure, so unadulterated, so perfect, and so righteous that if we go back to when you were first enlightened and had the revelation, to when you first believed in your heart, you felt so holy, you loved so much, you were in a paradise of wonderment. You had no desire for sin; sin had lost its desire.

There you were, with a New Birth unto righteousness, filled with the first love of purity and truth. You felt everyone was going to be saved and the world was going to be turned upside down, because you "had gotten it." That was the first touch .

It was a remarkable revelation to me when I first saw that God had purposed that every newborn babe in Christ was called to be a saint; called from the darkness to light, from the power of Satan unto God; separated at the revelation that Jesus is the Son of God.

God Has Predestined

Another fact was this: For days and days, something so remarkable came over your life that you neither had desire for nor did, sin.

Do you have a recollection of those moments? Praise God! God had designed the plan for you before the world was. I believe that God wants to open your heart and mind to a predestined condition of why you are here.

We want to be so established with facts that there won't be a thing in the world that is able to move us from our perfect position.

Can you say, though sin is striving about you, that you never remember a day when God did not strive with you? It is impossible to be in the world without satanic forces trying to bid loudly for your life. But can you say that, from your very infancy, you have always remembered that the good hand of God was with you? If you knew the Scriptures, you could say, like Paul, that God had called you from your mother's womb.

Beloved, God has predestined. There are two great words in the Scriptures: "whosoever will" and "whosoever won't" God has covered the world with His blood, and every man is redeemed, whether he will have it or not. But there are some people whom God has wonderfully chosen before the foundation of the world. And, as surely as we are here, we can say that God has predestined us even to this day.

Although you have been defeated, the tendency, and the longings, and the cryings, and the desires of your whole life have been, *you wanted God.*

See how much God has for you in the Word! God wants people who are mighty in the Spirit; who are full of power. God has no such thing as small measures for man. God has GREAT DESIGNS for man! God has determined by His power and His grace through the Son to bring many sons unto glory, clothed upon with the Holy One from heaven.

Tongues Interpretation

The Lord of life and glory, who has begotten us to a lively hope, hath chosen us before the foundation of the world, that He may manifest His Son in us and get glory over the powers of darkness and the devil—and EVERY evil thing—that we may reign over the powers of the devil.

Catch the Breath of the Spirit

The Holy Ghost is jealous over us this morning. How He longs for us to catch the breath of His Spirit! How He longs for us to be moved in union with Himself, that there may not be a thought in heaven but that the Holy Ghost would breathe through the natural, and so chasten it by His divine plan, that you would have a new faith or a revelation of God.

You would then be so perfect before God that there would not be a thing that Satan could say contrary to His child.

Hear what Satan said to God about Job: *"Hast not thou made an hedge about him?..."* (Job 1:10). God only said, *"...all that he hath is in thy power; only upon himself put not forth thine hand..."* (v. 12).

We see that God put a hedge about His child. Oh, that we would believe!

Hearken to what Jesus says: *"...do ye not remember? When I brake the five loaves among five thousand, how many baskets full of fragments took ye up? They say unto him, Twelve"* (Mark 8:18,19).

Oh, if we had not forgotten the blessings and the pressed-out measures, everything would be moved by the manifestation of the children of God! We would stand by the power of the righteousness of heaven and move the world!

"Who is he that overcomethth e world, but he that believeth that Jesus is the Son of God?" (1 John 5:5). It is most beautiful! *"For whatsoever is born of God overcometh the world: and this is the victory that overcometht he world, even our faith"* (v. 4). We shall have to come into divine measurement, divine revelation, of this. The possibilities are ours!

The Promise Is Yours

One day I was in Belfast, Ireland. I had a friend there they called "Morris." He had been with us at Bradford, and I wanted to see him, so I went to his house and asked, "Is Brother Morris here?"

The woman answered, "It is not Morris you want. God sent you for me. I am a brokenhearted woman. I am going through death, having the greatest trial of my life. Come in."

I went in. She continued, "My husband is a deacon in the Presbyterian church, and you know that when you were here, God filled me with the Holy Ghost. The Spirit of the Lord came upon me, and I was so filled with joy that I broke out in tongues. The whole church turned around to look at me for making such a disturbance."

At the close of the meeting, the deacons and the pastor came to her husband, saying, "You cannot be a deacon in this church because of your wife's behavior."

It nearly broke his heart. When he saw all his influence was to go, he came home in bitterness. He and his wife had lived together many years, and had never known a discord. After causing much trouble, he left his wife with the words, "I will never come near you again as long as I live."

After she told me the story, we prayed, and the power of God shook her. God showed me that He would give her all she required. "Mrs.—, wake up," I exclaimed. "Look, the situation is yours! It is according to the Word of God: *'For the unbelieving husband is sanctified by the wife, and the unbelieving wife is sanctified by the husband...For what knowest thou, O wife, whether thou shalt save thy husband? or how knowest thou, O man, whether thou shalt save thy wife?'* (1 Corinthians 7:14,16). You will be the means of your husband being saved and baptized."

"Yes," she replied, "if I could believe he will ever come back; but he will never come back."

"Look," I said, "the Word of God says, *'...if two of you shall agree on earth as touching any thing that they shall ask, it shall be done for them of my Father which is in heaven'* (Matthew 18:19). We will agree that he comes home tonight."

Tongues Interpretation

God has designed a purpose for His people. And the Word of truth comes to us by interpretation: 'Whatsoever thou shalt bind on earth shall be bound in heaven: and whatsoever thou shalt loose on earth shall be loosed in heaven" (Matthew 16:19).

I advised her, "When your husband comes home, show him you love him. It is possible that he won't have it. As soon as he retires, get down before God and get filled, just as you were here. Then touch him in God."

Her husband was obliged to come home. (Whatsoever you desire, if you believe God, comes to pass.) He marched up and down in the house, as though he never saw her, then retired to his room. Then she got down before God.

Oh, the place of all places, where God comes to the soul! The Holy Spirit came upon her until her whole being was filled with the flame of heaven. Then she touched him. He screamed, rolled off onto the floor, and cried for mercy. She never left him until he was filled with the Holy Ghost.

Nothing happens to the believer but that which is good for him. *"...all things work together for good to them that love God,"* but we must not forget this injunction *"to them who are the called according to his purpose"* (Romans 8:28).

Remember, you are called "according to His purpose"—the working out of the power of God within you for the salvation of others. God has a purpose for you!

Look, beloved, I want you to be without carefulness. How many people are bound and helpless, and their testimony is naught because of carefulness? Hear what the Scripture says: *"Thou hast hid these things from the wise and prudent, and hast revealed them unto babes. Even so, Father: for it seemed good in thy sight"* (Matthew 11:25, 26).

You Are a Child of God

The first thing that God does with a newborn child is to keep him as a child. There are wonderful things for children! The difference between a child and the wise and prudent is this: The prudent man is too careful. The wise man knows too much.

But the babies! We sometimes have had to pull the bottle back, lest they consume the bottle with the milk, they are so ravenous!

The child cannot dress itself, but God clothes it. He has a special raiment for children—white and beautiful. God says there is no spot on the child. He says, *"Thou art pure; thou art altogether lovely."*

The babe cannot talk. But it is lovely to know that you need take no thought about what you shall say, for the Holy Ghost can speak through you. If you are a child, and you give all over to God, He can speak through you.

He loves His children. Oh, how beautifully He sees to His children. How kind and good He is!

"Who is he that overcometh the world, but he that believeth that Jesus is the Son of God?" (1 John 5:5). That pure, that holy, that devoted Person who made the world submits His will to Almighty God, His Father. God uses His will, and God indwells Him in fullness.

Jesus meets the world's need. He comes in at the dry time, when there is no wine, and He makes the wine. Glory to God! When there is no bread, He comes in and makes the bread.

He who believes that Jesus is the Son of God overcomes the world. You ask, "How can a man overcome the world because he believes that Jesus is the Son of God?" Because Jesus is so holy, and you become His habitation.

Jesus is so sweet! His love passeth all understanding. His wisdom passeth all knowledge; therefore, He comes to you with the wisdom of God, not of this world.

He comes to you with peace, put not as this world giveth. He comes to you with boundless blessing; with a measure pressed down and running over.

You do not require food from the world, for you have "meat to eat that the world knows not of" God is a Rewarder of all who diligently seek Him, for those who seek Him shall lack no good thing (Psalm 34:10).

Brother, where are your bounds today? There are heights and depths and lengths and breadths to the love of God.

Beloved, the Word of God contains the principles of life. I live not, but Another mightier than I liveth. My desires have gone into the desires of God. It is lovely! It is a position so perfected in the Holy Ghost that God is continually bringing forth things both new and old!

How We Overcome

"Who is he that overcometh the world, but he that believeth that Jesus is the Son of God?" (1 John 5:5). How do we overcome? We may come into this great inheritance *of the Spirit.*

We long for there to be nothing in us which Satan could use in overcoming us. Remember the words of Jesus: *"The prince of this world cometh, and hath nothing in Me"* (John 14:30). We desire to reach such a place as this. Is it possible? Brother, it is the design of the Master!

Without holiness, no man shall see the Lord. *"...he that is begotten of God keepeth himself, and that wicked one toucheth him not"* (1 John 5:18).

Surely, the Lord is not going to send you away empty. He wants to satisfy your longing soul with good things.

"Whatsoever is born of God overcometh the world: and this is the victory that overcometh the world, even our faith" (1 John 5:4).

Let me speak about three classes of faith. There is a "good," there is a "better," and there is a "best." God has the best.

In Pentecostal circles, I find some people are satisfied with "tongues." That would never satisfy me. I want the Person who gives them! I am the hungriest man you ever saw. I want all He has. Unless God gives to me, I am a perfectly spoiled baby. "Father," I say, "You will have to give to me."

When I was a little boy, I would go to my father and say, "Father, will you give me some bird lime?"

"No, no," he would answer.

I knew just what he meant from the way he said it. I would plead, "Father, Father, Father, Father!"

I would follow him as he walked out. "Father, Father, Father!"

Mother would ask, "Why don't you give the lad what he wants?"

I got to the place where I believed my father liked me to say it. If you only knew how God likes to hear us say, "Father, my Father!" Oh, how He loves His children!

I will never forget when we had our first baby. He was asleep in the cradle. We both went to him, and my wife said, "I cannot bear to have him sleep any longer. I want him!"

And I remember waking the baby, because she wanted him.

"If ye then, being evil, know how to give good gifts unto your children: how much more shall your heavenly Father give the Holy Spirit to them that ask Him?" (Luke 11:13). Ah, He is such a lovely Father!

"But," you say, "sometimes I give in."

Never mind; I am going to bring you to a point where you need never give in. Praise God! If I did not know the mighty power of

God, I would jump off this platform. Because we are quickened and made alive, we move into the new spirit, the spirit of fellowship, that was lost in the garden. Oh, hallelujah! New birth! New life! A new person!

Faith That Does Not Fail

Human faith works and then waits for the wages. That is not saving faith. Then there is *the gift of faith*. *"For by grace are ye saved through faith; and that not of yourselves: it is the gift of God"* (Ephesians 2:8). Faith is that which God gave you to believe. *"Whosoever believeth that Jesus is the Christ is born of God..."* (1 John 5:1). The sacrifice is complete, and God has kept you because you could not keep yourself.

I want to tell you of something that does not fail. Let us read in Acts 26:

> But rise, and stand upon thy feet: for I have appeared unto thee for this purpose, to make thee a minister and a witness both of these things which thou hast seen, and of those things in the which I will appear unto thee;
>
> Delivering thee from the people, and from the Gentiles, unto whom now I send thee,
>
> To open their eyes, and to turn them from darkness to light, and from the power of Satan unto God, that they may receive forgiveness of sins, and inheritance among them which are sanctified by faith that is in Me.
>
> Acts 26:16-18

That is "another faith." In First Corinthians 12:9, we read, *"To another faith by the same Spirit...."* When my faith fails, then "another faith" lays hold of me!

One day I called at a home where a woman had not slept for seven weeks. She was rolling from one side of the bed to the other. In came a young man with a baby in his arms. He stooped down over the mother to try to kiss her. Instantly, she rolled to the other side of the bed. Going around to her, the young man touched the lips of the mother with the baby to bring consciousness again. I could see that the young man was brokenhearted.

"What have you done for this woman?" I asked.

"Everything," they replied. "We have had doctors here, injected morphine, and so forth."

The sister said, "We must put her in an asylum. I am tired and worn out."

I asked, "Have you tried God?"

The husband answered, "Do you think we believe in God here? We have no confidence in anything. If you call anything like this God, we have no fellowship with it."

Oh, I was done then! A young woman then grinned in my face and slammed the door.

The compassion in me was so moved, I did not know what to do. I began to cry, and my faith took me right up. Thank God for faith that lifted! I felt Another grip me like the Son of God. The Spirit of the Lord came upon me, and I said, "In the Name of Jesus, come out of her!"

She fell asleep and did not wake for 14 hours. She wakened perfectly sane.

Brother, there is a place to know the Son of God, that absolutely overcomes the world!

One time I thought I had the Holy Ghost. Now I know the Holy Ghost has got *me*. There is a difference between our hanging on to God and God lifting us up. There is a difference between my having a desire and God's desire filling my soul. There is a difference between natural compassion and the compassion of Jesus that never fails. Human faith fails; but the faith of Jesus never fails!

Oh, beloved, I see through these glorious truths a new dawning: assemblies loving one another, all of one accord. Until that time comes, there will be deficiencies.

Hear what the Scripture says: *"...every one that loveth him that "begat loveth him also that is begotten of him"* (1 John 5:1). Also, Jesus said, *"By this shall all men know that ye are my disciples, if ye have love one to another"* (John 13:35).

Love is the secret and center of the divine position, "Build upon God."

The Gift of Faith

You ask, "What is the gift of faith?"

It is where God moves you to pray.

Elijah was a man with like passions as we have. The sins of the people were grieving the heart of God, and the whole house of Ahab was in an evil state.

But God moved upon this man and gave him an inward cry: *"...there shall not be dew nor rain these years, but according to my word"* (1 Kings 17:1), the Word says, *"...and it rained not on the earth by the space of three years and six months"* (James 5:17).

Oh, if we dared to believe God! A man of like passions as we have was stirred with almightiness! *"And he prayed again, and the heaven gave rain, and the earth brought forth her fruit"* (James 5:18).

Brother, sister, you are now in the robing room. God is adding another day for you to come into line; for you to lay aside everything that has hindered you; for you to forget the past.

And I ask you: Do you want to touch God for a faith that cannot be denied? I have learned this: that if I dare put out my hands in faith, God will fill them.

Come on, beloved, seek God, and let us get a real touch of heaven today! God is moving! This day is the beginning of days—a day when the Lord will not forsake His own. He will meet us. Come near to God!

I pray, *"Jesus, Jesus, bless us! We are so needy, Lord. Jesus, my Lord! Oh, Jesus, Jesus, Jesus! Oh, my Savior, my Savior! Oh, such love! Thou mighty God! Oh, loving Master! Blessed, blessed Jesus! None like Jesus! None so good as He! None so sweet as He! Oh, thou blessed Christ of reality, come! Hallelujah!"*

(California, June 3, 1924, issued by Glad Tidings Tabernacle and Bible Institute, San Francisco)

Chapter 11

Revival

R evival is coming! God is coming forth with power! The latter rain is appearing!

At this time, there must be no coming down from the cross, but a going on from faith to faith and from glory to glory, with an increasing diligence to be found in Him blameless and without spot (2 Peter 3:14).

God's heart is in the place of intense passion. Let us bend or break, for God is determined to bless us. Oh, the joy of service and the joy of suffering—the joy of being utterly cast upon Jesus!

A divine plan is outworking:

> *...Behold, the husbandman waiteth for the precious fruit of the earth,...until he receive the early and latter rain.*
>
> James 5:7

Jesus is wanting to give the early and the latter rain and see the precious fruit taken in. Jesus is wanting to do it all!

A Sown Life

Worship is higher than fellowship. Oh, the calmness of meeting with Jesus! All fears are gone. His tender mercy and indescribable peace are ours.

I have all if I have *Jesus* pruning the tree, for if there is a pruning by Him, more fruit can grow. All God's plans for us are at the end of a yielded will. James 5:7 says that God is waiting for the precious *fruit* of the earth, the outcome of a sown life. Nothing is more divine or lovelier.

The seed has to die. It has to be sown for a great harvest to come.

Great was the day of Jezreel, whom God sowed. In his day, there was *"one head"* (Hosea 1:11). We have one Head over us, too: Jesus!

> *...I will break the bow of Israel in the valley of Jezreel* [whom God sows; the seed of God].
>
> *...I will break the bow and the sword and the battle out of the earth...*
>
> *And I will betroth thee unto me...in righteousness, and in judgment, and in lovingkindness, and in mercies.*
>
> *I will even betroth thee unto me in faithfulness: and thou shalt know the Lord.*
>
> *...I will hear the heavens* [saying, "Sit with me!"] *and they shall hear the earth* [this company shall hear the groaning of the people];
>
> *And the earth shall hear the com, and the* [new] *wine, and the oil; and they shall hear Jezreel* [the seed of God].
>
> Hosea 1:5; 2:18-22

Amen! Let the people hear. Let God do as He has promised.

God awaits the death of the seed, for it springs into LIFE. And how do you know the seed is dead? Why, the green shoots appear. God awaits the evidence of death before that which Isaiah 11 speaks of can appear: a place of profound rest (v. 10). It is a place of comfort. Jesus said, *"I will pray the Father, and he shall give you another Comforter..."* (John 14:16).

Not a sound invades the stillness,
Not a form invades the scene,
Save the voice of my Beloved
And the person of my King.

Precious, gentle, holy Jesus,
Blessed Bridegroom of my heart,
In thy secret inner chamber
Thou wilt whisper what Thou art.

And within those heavenly places
Calmly hushed in sweet repose,
There I drink with jay absorbing
And the love Thou wouldst disclose.

Wrapped in deep, adoring silence,
Jesus, Lord, I dare not move
Lest I lose the smallest saying
Meant to catch the ear of love.

Rest then, oh, my soul, contented,
Thou hast reached that happy place—
In the bosom of thy Savior,
Gazing up in His dear face.

The Early and Latter Rains

The early and the latter rains appear. The early rain is to make the seed die, to come to an end, leaving it as ashes. And out of the ashes comes the great fire of consummation that shall burn in the hearts of the people the Word of the living God, producing the Christ in us by the breath of the Spirit.

First, ashes; then the latter rain appears. It is a surging of *life*. The old is finished. The early rain had been to get us ready for that which was to come.

Now on those who know the Father, a surging life flows forth. Mark 16 tells of the signs following those who believe; it is a mighty and glorious outpouring. The effect of the latter rain is *a universal outpouring of the Holy Spirit.*

The coming of the Lord is at hand; the Judge is standing at the door (James 5:8,9)! Has His Spirit come?

> *When he is come, he will reprove* [convict] *the world* [convincing men] *of sin,...*
>
> *Of judgment, because the prince of this world is judged.*
>
> John 16:8, 11

Jesus said:

> *...if I depart, I will send him unto you.*
>
> John 16:7

Men are being convicted. Jesus has departed. YES, He has come!

The baptism of the Holy Spirit is for the death of the seed. The Holy Ghost wakes up every passion in us, permitting every trial. His object is to make the vessel pure. All must "die" before a manifestation of God unthought of, undreamt of, comes. That's why God is waiting to move and shake all that can be shaken.

Be "killed." Be prepared—a vessel to pour out torrents!

A Call to Martyrdom

It's a call to martyrdom, to death of spirit, soul, and body. *To the death!* The choice is before you. Decide to accept the path for death to life. Such absolute abandonment is necessary for receiving divine equipment for the early and the latter rains' appearing.

Isaiah 11, which speaks of the Spirit, is God's equipment for the understanding of the worldwide purposes of God. It speaks of a time when,

> *...the earth shall be full of the knowledge of the Lord, as the waters cover the sea.*
>
> Isaiah 11:9

Knowledge of the loveliness of Jesus and the glory of God is revelation to a perishing world. It is a *"perishing"* world, because *"Where there is no vision, the people perish..."* (Proverbs 29:18).

Wake up! The air is full of revival. We look for a mighty outpouring that will shake all that can be shaken.

Take all else, but give me vision and revelation of the purposes of God! Give me a wonderful, burning love—the love of Jesus!

Oh, yes, it must come—uttermost death for uttermost life. The early AND the latter rains appear. We count those happy that endure the first to receive the second. Count it not strange, beloved—the fiery breath of revival IS coming! There is a ripple on the lake; a murmur in the air.

The price for it is tremendous: *It is martyrdom.* We must seal the testimony with our "blood." There must be an outworking of the cross—a dying, searching, and crucifying, with no resisting.

Jesus says, "Trust Me. *'It is finished'*" (John 19:30).

First, sow your life. Then the revelation of God, with eternal issues for multitudes, comes. The *latter* rain appears. All are moved before the men of God have moved; millions are gathered into the kingdom. And the heart of God is satisfied!

> *Since thou art come to that holy room*
> *Where with the choirs of saints forevermore,*
> *Thou art made my music;*
> *Thine, the instrument, here at the door—*
> *And what thou must do*
> *Then think here before.*

(Date and place of sermon unknown.)

Chapter 12

The Secret Place

He that dwelleth in the secret place of the most High shall abide under the shadow of the Almighty.

I will say of the Lord, He is my refuge and my fortress: my God; in him will I trust.

Surely he shall deliver thee from the snare of the fowler, and from the noisome pestilence.

He shall cover thee with his feathers, and under his wings shalt thou trust: his truth shall be thy shield and buckler.

Thou shalt not be afraid for the terror by night; nor for the arrow that flieth by day;

Nor for the pestilence that walketh in darkness; nor for the destruction that wasteth at noonday.

A thousand shall fall at thy side, and ten thousand at thy right hand; but it shall not come nigh thee.

Only with thine eyes shalt thou behold and see the reward of the wicked.

Because thou hast made the Lord, which is my refuge, even the most High, thy habitation;

There shall no evil befall thee, neither shall any plague come nigh thy dwelling.

For he shall give his angels charge over thee, to keep thee in all thy ways.

They shall bear thee up in their hands, lest thou dash thy foot against a stone.

Thou shalt tread upon the lion and adder: the young lion and the dragon shalt thou trample under feet.

Because he hath set his love upon me, therefore will I deliver him: I will set him on high, because he hath known my name.

He shall call upon me, and I will answer him: I will be with him in trouble; I will deliver him, and honour him.

With long life will I satisfy him, and shew him my salvation.

Psalm 91

The crown of life is for the overcomer. It is not for those at ease in Zion. We must be in the place where God can depend upon us to keep going until we see victory, never giving in and knowing no defeat, always making our stand by a living faith and gaining the victory. Faith is the victory.

This is the work of God, that ye believe on him whom he hath sent.

John 6:29

England once had a war with France. Some prisoners were taken; among them, a drummer boy. Napoleon ordered him to sound a retreat. He said, "No!" He had never learned one.

God never wants you to retreat before the enemy, but to learn the song of victory and overcome! Praise the Lord!

There are two kinds of shouts: a shout that is made, and a shout that makes you. There are men of God, but there are also men who are God's men. There is a place where you take hold of God, but there is a better place where God takes hold of you.

Psalm 91:1 says, *"He that dwelleth in the secret place of the most High shall abide under the shadow of the Almighty."* Do YOU know the presence of the Almighty? It is wonderful. It is a surety, with no wavering, no unbelief, no unrest there. It is perfect!

Fear the Lord

My great desire is to see men become strong in the Lord by dwelling in the secret place, which is known to all who fear Him.

Now, there are two kinds of fear. One fear involves being afraid of God. I hope you are not there. Unbelievers are there. But the believer should desire, rather, to die than to grieve God by fearing Him in this way.

Fellowship with God, peace, and power—this is God's will for us, so don't fear that it isn't. No price is too great to pay to have it. It is our inheritance. *Christ* purchased it for us. Through Him we have the covering of the presence of the Almighty. What a covering the unfolding of His will is!

The secret place of the Lord is with those who fear Him in the second way: with respect and honor. Moses knew something about it. He feared God and said to Him, *"If thy presence go not with me, carry us not up hence"* (Exodus 33:15).

Oh, to dwell in the secret place, His presence! What will this presence do? It will dare us to believe all God says, assisting us to lay hold of the promises. We will have God so indwelling us that we will become a force, a power of God's abiding, until the time death is swallowed up in victory!

We have a great salvation filled with inspiration. It has no limitations; it makes known the immeasurable wonders of God.

If you are in the experience of verse 1, here is an added substance of faith for you. (It is a *fact*. And you need to have facts, inward facts, instead of "fearings" or feelings, because you will be beyond anyone's argument when you have them.) There are those who proclaim, *"I will say of the Lord, he is my refuge and my fortress: my God; in him will I trust"* (Psalm 91:2). Who will say it? He that abideth! He who abides in the Lord knows he can trust in the Lord to protect him from harm.

Free From the Law of Sin and Death

There is no "kick" in the secret place—no evil temper, no irritability. All is swept away while one is dwelling in the presence of the Almighty; in the covering of God. Even the best of humanity, when from the devil, is not good, and cannot remain in God's presence. Jesus was manifested to destroy ALL the works of the devil (1 John 3:8).

> *For what the law could not do, in that it was weak*
> *through the flesh, God sending his own Son in the*

likeness of sinful flesh, and for sin, condemned sin in the flesh.

Romans 8:3

God sent forth Jesus in the mightiness of His power. In flesh and in the midst of flesh, He condemned it. The law of the Spirit of life was destroying *all* that must be destroyed. Dead indeed unto sin, but alive unto God, we then are above all in Him: He that is above all and through all and in you all.

This is a fact, not in human nature, but in God. It is the gift of God from heaven. We belong to the new creation, and we are in a wonderful place in life. It is a life free from the law of sin and death.

Can we keep ourselves there? GOD can keep us there.

> *He never forgets to keep me,*
> *He never forgets to keep me.*
> *My Father has many dear children;*
> *But He never forgets to keep me.*

Has He forgotten to keep *you*? Nay! He cannot forget. God has much in store for you; you are far from being out of His thoughts.

God's Word: Antidote to Evil

There was a time when the children of Israel hung their harps on the willows in defeat. Sometimes the believer does the same. The song of joy leaves his heart. It doesn't have to happen. I have seen thousands delivered from evil powers.

You must be aware that there is a great weakness in the land: It is a *lack of knowledge.* People hew out cisterns that can hold no water, instead of filling themselves with the Word of God.

There is NO fear like the Israelites experienced in the face of their enemy for those who know the Word of God. God's Word is the great antidote to evil.

You see, *"There is no fear in love; but perfect love casteth out fear..."* (1 John 4:18). And where is God, who is Love? He is in the Word. He has embodied Himself in the Word. The Word spells destruction to all evil, because God is in the Word, and He is greater than all evil. Therefore, *he that dwelleth in love is master of evil situations.* He that dwelleth in GOD, in His presence and in His Word, is master of evil situations. We have no fear! We are over every sickness! Ours is a perfect redemption!

Concerning the healing Christ secured for us in redemption, some ask, "Does it last? Does the healing stand good?" Yes! What God does, He does to last forever!

Many years ago, God healed me when all my teeth were decayed and weak. God healed them when I was sixty-two. I am as fresh as a boy! *Now, devil, take THAT!* Such healing is God's plan, which is better than any other plan!

Some turn from God's plan because of fear. Others throw over God's wonderful plan because of a feeling. The Bible has so many precious promises, with wealth beyond all price, that God has planned for us to have. Seek after God's plan. Don't be unbelieving, for the waverer gets nothing. Real faith is established, never changing, and with it you'll get all God has for you.

Established Faith

"How can I get established faith?" you ask.

Abide under the shadow of the Almighty. Don't change your position, but always have the presence of God, the glory of God. Pay any price to abide under that covering, for the secret of victory is to abide where the Victor abides.

Higher, higher, nothing dreading

Never, never let me stop;

In thy footsteps keep my treading

Give me strength to reach the top.

Jesus has become the Author and the Finisher of your faith. Through faith in Him, you came to the Father, *"For with the heart man believeth unto righteousness; and with the mouth confession is made unto salvation"* (Romans 10:10). Your life is hid with Christ in God. You have no limitation when the holy breath blows an inward cry after Him.

Oh, do you know His Name? If you do, God will set you on high (Psalm 91:14). And you can ask what you will—communion with Jesus, fellowship divine—and it shall be given to you. It comes through knowledge of Jesus' Name, not just by whispering it now and then.

Call upon the Lord, and He will answer you (Psalm 91:15). Feed upon His Word. To those who do, God has said, *"With long life will I satisfy him, and shew him my salvation"* (Psalm 91:16). Amen.

(Switzerland, August 1921)

Chapter 13

The Moving Breath of the Spirit

The Word is God Himself.

In the beginning was the Word, and the Word was with God, and the Word was God.

John 1:1

This creates in us an attitude of rest, because all our hope is in the Word of the living God. The Word of God abideth forever; it is *always* able to help us. Oh, the glorious truths found therein!

Never compare this book with other books. This book is from heaven. It does not contain the Word of God; it IS the Word of God. It is supernatural in origin, eternal in duration and value, infinite in scope, and divine in authorship.

Read it through!

Pray it in!

Write it down!

And what does the Word say? It says, *"The fear of the Lord is the beginning of wisdom..."* (Proverbs 9:10). In the fear of the Lord we begin to realize our weakness, which moves us to wisely receive the greatness of redemption. Knowledge is coupled with joy. We cannot have the knowledge of the Lord *without* joy.

Not only do we have joy; we have peace. Faith brings peace. Not faith through long petitions, but faith by grace brings peace. Peace is found where faith is undisturbed (unchanged, unaffected). That is eternal faith—daring always to believe what God has said.

If you'll dare to trust Him, you'll find your desire always comes to pass. But there must be no wavering, for *"... let not that man think he shall receive any thing of the Lord"* (James 1:7).

ONLY BELIEVE!

Become an Expression of the King

Jesus being full of the Holy Ghost returned from Jordan....

Luke 4:1

What does it really mean to *"... be filled with the Spirit,"* like Ephesians 5:18 tells us? We all need to know. Oh, the difference it makes when we understand the baptism of the Holy Spirit and know the flow of the life of the Spirit! How the Word becomes illuminated by the Spirit! We leap for joy, beyond anything we have ever done before, with holy laughter!

Out of the shadow, the reality of the substance, that infilling of the Spirit which had been promised, has come. Our glorious Lord, who can speak as no other, is here to help the oppressed!

The King unfolds His will. He covers His child, flooding the soul with open vision; with untiring zeal. Fire! Fire! Fire! It burns intensely in the human soul, until the person becomes an expression of the King!

I know the Lord laid His hand on me;
He filled me with the Holy Ghost.
I know the Lord laid His hand on me.

This Jesus, this wonder-working Jesus, came to be King. Is He King? Yes! And He must reign in our lives. Oh, to so yield that He always has the first place! Glory be to God! His Spirit has come to abide forever, flooding our souls, for Jesus said, "When I go, I will send Him unto you" (John 16:7, paraphrased).

Has He come to you?
Has He come to you?
Has the Comforter come to you?

The Lord said that He will reprove the world of sin when the Comforter comes to us. God has given us an enrichment, a perfection of revelation, in Him. The Spirit came to fill the Body and to bring forth that which all the prophets had spoken of, taking of the things of Jesus and showing them unto us.

Filled With the Spirit

The woman in John 4 had a well. After the Holy Ghost had come, she had a river. Rivers of living water began to flow out of her.

A prophetic utterance is part of the infilling of the Spirit, and it flows like a river. It is a divine incoming, helping to fill the Body unto all the fullness of God. It is like a flash of lightning, opening up divine revelation.

By it, we realize we can dance and sing in the Spirit. We can enjoy sweeter music and rarity of character (the character of Christ in us, the hope of glory). We see a vision of the glory of God in the face of Jesus Christ. These divine revelations are what the baptism of the Holy Spirit brings to us through prophecy and other means.

The Holy Spirit is the Spirit of Truth. He is ever unveiling, making manifest, breathing upon humanity in a great way, burning, quickening, until men cry out, "What must we do to be saved?" So comes the breath of life, burning with intensity until the world feels the warmth and cries out for God.

Oh, the joy of being filled with the Holy Ghost and having the divine purpose of taking His fire to the world! We must have such activity in season and out of season, with the sense of divine approval!

As the apostles were in their day, we are to be in our day: filled unto all the fullness of God, with the same Holy Ghost, the same warmth, the same life—*the same heaven in the soul.*

The Holy Ghost brings heaven to us as He reveals Jesus, who is the King of heaven. Oh, the perfection of belonging to Him in whom we have a heavenly preparation for every need!

There is no need to groan, cry, travail, or sigh. The Word says:

The Spirit of the Lord is upon me....

Luke 4:18

We have the Spirit of the Lord. We have the sense of the Holy Ghost, the knowledge of His power, the sweetness of His experience, the wonder of His breath. He is lifting the Word, making all things new, meeting the present need in our lives.

These are the last days. They are very wonderful and blessed with signs. The breath of the Spirit is unfolding God's truths and helping mankind to know Jesus.

Enforcement of Expression

I believe in the Holy Ghost. And I believe that God gave us the Holy Ghost for true Son-likeness, Son-expressiveness, and *enforcement* of that expression.

In Sweden, a large platform was erected in a park for meetings on the condition that this Englishman would not put his hands on the people and pray.

I said, "Lord, You know all about this. I believe You can work."

The Lord revealed His presence and healed and saved the people anyway at the meetings. I simply said, "Who here is in need? Put your hands up."

Hands went up all over. I saw a large woman with her hand up. I said, "Tell your trouble!"

She said that pains were all over her body. She was in terrible distress. I said, "Lift up your hands in Jesus' Name!"

Jesus came to heal the sick, to loose those the devil had bound, to set the captives free. He said, "GREATER works than these shall you who believe on me do" (John 14:12, paraphrased).

We have the power of His Name to use against the enemy. I said to the woman, "In the Name of Jesus, I set you free. Are you freer."

She replied, "Yes, perfectly free!"

GOD put His hands on the people! He had wonderful ways of meeting the need there.

I *believe* to see the glory of God. I *believe* to see God setting people free from all weakness.

Making Disciples of All Nations

Jesus said, *"The Spirit of the Lord is upon me…to make disciples of all nations"* (Luke 4:18; Matthew 28:19, paraphrased).

In New Zealand, when I first preached this glorious truth, I saw hundreds baptized. In Sweden, however, the Lutheran church was not pleased. A woman in the king's household was healed, but I was forced to leave the country.

On one occasion there, I stayed on a side street. I arrived at nine-thirty; but the meeting was not until four-thirty, so I went to the coast for a few hours of rest. When I came back, the street was full from end to end with wheelchairs and cars filled with the helpless and needy. The conveners said, "What shall we do?"

I said, "The Holy Ghost came to abide, to reign in supreme royal dignity. Live in His unction, freedom, inspiration, and be like a flowing river—nothing less—that God may be glorified."

God loosed the people that day and brought deliverance to the captives. Was that all that happened? No, only the beginning! The house I was at was packed, too!

Oh, the joy of being ready for God to use us! God must set us all on fire. There is much land to be possessed, and we must possess it. The fields are white unto harvest!

Oh, the cry of the people that day—talk about weeping! There is such a joy in weeping. It is an awful place if you cannot weep with the breath of God upon you as they did that day.

I went on helping the people. God said to me as dearly as possible, *Ask Me! I will give you all in the place.*

I thought it was too big a request to ask. He whispered again, *Ask! I will give you all in the house.*

I said, "O my God, say it again."

Ask of Me. I will give you all in the house.

I said, "I ask! I ask in faith! I believe it!"

The breath of heaven filled the place. The people continued to fall down, weeping and repenting.

Oh, the breath of the Spirit! There is something WONDERFUL in this breath!

The Spirit Is Upon ME

Jesus said, *"The Spirit of the Lord is upon me..."* (Luke 4:18).

"And it is upon me, upon ME" we can say.

May God move in our hearts to act in this truth. Do you want God to have you in His splendid place of the moving of His Spirit? Is it the cry and the longing of your heart to come to this place? God can only choose those filled to the uttermost to be there. Do you long to be filled to the uttermost; are you hungering and thirsting after God's fullness? Stand in a living experience, as Jesus did. Say, "The Spirit of the Lord is upon ME!" and what you desire will happen.

God grant it to every one of you. Amen.

(August 1925)

Chapter 14

Preparation for the Rapture

Our hearts are moved. God is moving us to believe that He is on the throne, waiting for us to make application. Stretch out your hands to God to believe that the almightiness of His grace is for us in a most marvelous way. Whatever yesterday was, today is to be greater.

Are you ready? What for? To come to a place where you will not give way; a place where you will dare believe that God is the same today as He was yesterday, and will surely make you satisfied, because He longs to fill you. Those who believe shall be satisfied.

Are you ready? What for? To so apply your heart to the will of God, to so yield yourself to the purposes of God, that God will work a plan through your life that has never been before.

Are you ready? What for? To come into such like-mindedness with Christ today that you have no more human desire, but you will be cut short from all human bondages and be set free. The shoreline must never again know you. Come to God in all the depths of His fullness, His revelation, His power, that you may today be clothed upon with God.

I believe that you believe in the coming of the Lord and the Rapture which is to take place. I am going to deal with the position that leads you right up to the Rapture. To that end, we will be reading the fifth chapter of Second Corinthians.

This is one of those divine propositions. It is one of those openings to the heart that bring enlargement and conception. It is one of those moments that we enter into by faith to see that we can be so occupied, so changed, so in Christ, so ready, so clothed upon, so filled with Him, that the very breath of the life of that which is causing it would cause us to leave this earth.

Dead to Sin; Alive Unto God

As you listen to the Word, do not allow natural to interfere with supernatural evidences. You will never be what God has ordered you to be until you are willing to denounce your own failings, unbelief, and every human standard.

You must be willing to denounce them so that you might stand in place, complete, believing that you are a new creation in the Spirit; and that God, in a mighty way, can so fill you with life and destroy all that is natural that would interfere with the process of change, until you are alive unto God by the Spirit, ready for the coming of the Lord.

Now, we have here a definite position, as Paul had. Paul received much revelation which was clear to him, but not as clear to others. In fact, Peter said that Paul said many things which are hard to understand (2 Peter 3:16). "Nevertheless," Peter said, "we know they are of the Lord" (2 Peter 3:15, paraphrased).

Paul wrote many things that are hard to understand. Unless you are spiritually enlightened, you will not be able to comprehend the attitude of the place of ascension he had reached.

All your spiritual acquaintances should come into the place of ascension. Always keep in mind that to be conformed to this world is loss, but to be transformed from this world is gain. The transforming is the working of His mighty power in the mind.

The body and the soul can be so preserved in this wonderful life of God that nothing can hinder us from living as those who are dead to sin and alive unto God. We find that sin has been destroyed; disease, absolutely put aside; death, abolished in the life of the resurrection of Christ in the body!

The Spirit of the Lord is giving us revelation that will teach us a plan which is so supernatural, you will live absolutely in a new creation, if you dare believe. You will go by leaps and bounds into all the treasury of the Most High as you believe.

Nothing will interfere with you but yourself. And I believe God can change even your mind. He can give you much aspiration, holy-inflating life divine in human order, filling you with great ambition for purity, holiness, and transformation (which means "transportation").

God often has to cause revolution in the body before He can get the throne in a heart. He causes you to come to death, and then to death, and then to death, so you will see that sin violates, or hinders, progress; that anything of the natural order is not divine; that you have to have a divine mind (a new mind, a new will); that everything about you must be in the line of consecration, or separation unto perfection.

Believe it. Maybe as you examine yourself, you will believe it never could happen in your life. Get your mind off yourself—that is destruction. Get your mind on the Lord.

No building could be built without a plumb line and a straight edge. The Word of God is a true plumb line. God has given us a plumb line and a straight edge, causing us to be built in supernatural lines so that we may be an edifice in the Spirit, and causing us to be strong against the devil.

Tongues Interpretation

Weakness may be turned into power; feeblemindedness into the mind of Christ. The whole Body, fitly joined together in the Spirit, can rise and rise until it is an edifice in the Holy Ghost. It is not what it is; it is what it is going to be.

God has made preparation for us to be freed from the law of sin and death. He has gained the victory. He has overcome and vanquished the enemy, and the last enemy that shall be destroyed is death.

Yes, deeper, deeper and higher, higher we are to go; holier, holier and purer, purer we are to be—all until God sets His seal upon us. We are His forever, bought with a price—not with silver and gold, but with the precious blood.

Let the Spirit move thee, chasten thee, bring thee to naught. Thou must be chastened by the Lord in order to have the fruits of His holiness. He observes thee today to see if you live by the position "Except thou die, thou canst not live." (See John 12:24,25.)

While you are in the very attitude of death, He causes resurrection force to come into thy life until thou dost come out of all things into the living heart; until Christ is over thee, nourishing thee in the mind and in the body, and causing thy spirit to live; until thou dost feel the very breath of heaven breathing upon thee and the wings of the Spirit moving within thee.

Getting Ready for the Future Exit

For we know that if our earthly house of this tabernacle were dissolved, we have a building of God, an house not made with hands, eternal in the heavens.

For in this we groan, earnestly desiring to be clothed upon with our house which is from heaven.

2 Corinthians 5:1, 2

These verses speak of a present-tense lesson which makes us ready for a future exit. Present-tense lessons are wonderful. You miss a great deal if you do not live in the present tense. You must never put anything off until tomorrow. Believe God to work TODAY. He can do it. The Word of God says, *"Jesus Christ the same yesterday, and to day, and for ever"* (Hebrews 13:8).

Don't say, "Tomorrow I will be healed."

Don't say, "Tomorrow I will be baptized."

Don't say, "Tomorrow I will have more light."

"Today if you will hear His voice, harden not your hearts" (Hebrews 3:15, paraphrased), for the hearing of faith is wonderful! God wants you to believe and have everything TODAY!

We all wish that from this day on; no one would die. Speaking of death, the Scriptures say of the natural body, *"It is sown in dishonour..."* (1 Corinthians 15:43). We know that God is going to raise us in power, but there is a state we can go on to where we see that sin, disease, and death are destroyed, and we will live forever with the Lord.

Surpassing Joy

I want to help you today. If you are not moved in some way by this message, God is not with you. One of two things has to be: Either you have to be moved until you cannot rest, or you have to be made so glad, you cannot remain in the same place.

I cannot believe that anybody filled with the Spirit could speak to an assembly of people and they would be the same after he had finished. I take it for granted that God has me preaching to move you, to make you very thirsty, or to cause a gladness to come into your heart that will absolutely surpass everything else on the line of joy!

The Body Must Be Changed

No flesh can come into the presence of God. If you do die, a process occurs to get rid of all that is in the body. The very body that you are in must be disposed of. It must come to ashes.

There is no such thing as your body being in the presence of God. But if no flesh can come into the presence of God, then what is going into the presence of God? Your body has to give place to a *resurrection order;* to a *resurrection life.*

The Scriptures speak about dissolving. If your body does *not* go through the process of death and lose all the elements of earthly cabbages, potatoes, corn, wheat, and such—if it does *not* get rid of all its earthly acquaintances, but simply goes up—God will cause the old body to be turned into gases. There will not be a bit of it left.

In that moment, the very nature of Christ, the life of God in you, will be clothed upon with a body that can stand all eternity.

Be ready for a change. You say, "How can I be ready?"

I am going to answer that. Follow me very closely.

"For in this we groan,..." Second Corinthians 5:2 says. There should be a groaning attitude in us. We must reach a place where we see that there is some defect, that there is not a perfect purifying going on in our lives. When we come to that attitude—knowing we are bound—we will groan to be delivered.

What is this deliverance? Shall it come in this present world? Certainly. I am not in heaven yet; I am on the earth. I am dealing with people who are on the earth; people who can be on the earth and have supernatural power abounding within them.

The very nature that came into you when you were born again is of a spiritual quality of the nature of knowledge. It can understand supernatural things. It has power to compare spiritual things with spiritual things; and only those who are born of God can understand spiritual things. The world that has never been saved cannot understand them.

But the moment we are quickened, born again, made anew— this nature taking on its supernatural power—it begins travailing, groaning, to be delivered from the body. And it will go on, and cry on, and cry on, until the saints will be seen in large numbers, crying, "Come, Lord Jesus!"

The consummation will be most remarkable! But I believe God has a plan for us even before that occurs. Carefully and thoughtfully enter with me into more of the fifth chapter of Second Corinthians 5.

If so be that being clothed we shall not be found naked.

For we that are in this tabernacle do groan, being burdened: not for that we would be unclothed, but clothed upon, that mortality might be swallowed up of life.

2 Corinthians 5:3,4

I am dealing with clothing again. The first time, it was about being clothed *with flesh;* this time, it is about being clothed *with the Spirit.*

Being "clothed upon" in this way is not desiring to go, but desiring to *stop,* because we realize we are not exactly ready to go. We want to be so clothed upon *while* we are in the body—clothed upon with the life from heaven—that no natural thing would be in evidence in us. We then would be absolutely made alive in Christ, living only for the glory and the exhibition of the Lord of life.

This is the clothing we want, that we might not be naked. You know exactly what nakedness is. They knew when Jesus walked about, for their nakedness was made bare.

Nakedness is "a sense of consciousness that there is something that has not been dealt with, that has not been judged; hence, the blood has not had its perfect application."

Nakedness means that you are inwardly conscious that there is some hidden thing; something that has not been absolutely brought to the blood; something that could not possibly stand in God's presence; something that is not ready for the absolute glory.

Second Corinthians 5:4 also speaks of "life." The Word of life is preached unto you through the Gospel, and it has a wonderful power in it. It brings immortality into that which is natural in a person, until he realizes the first spring in his heart of supernatural power. And from that moment, he knows that he is in the earth, but he belongs to heaven, and that this life which is in him is a life which has power to eat up mortality.

Life That Eats Up Mortality

Two verses from the eighth chapter of Romans will help us here.

> *There is therefore now no condemnation to them which are in Christ Jesus, who walk not after the flesh, but after the Spirit.*
> *For the law of the Spirit of life...*

Romans 8:1, 2

The "Law of life" is that law which came into you which is incorruptible and divine. It is the very nature of the Son of God.

Suppose I was dealing with the subject of the coming of the Lord. The revelation that I have about the coming of the Lord is that all those who are going to be caught up are going to be eaten up. Their old nature, their old desires, their old life, is going to be eaten up by the life of Jesus Christ. When He comes, the life will meet THE Life; but the process we are going through now is for building you on the lines of readiness.

Yes, there is a life that has power to eat up mortality. What is mortality? When I speak about mortality, you no doubt think of your physical body and say, "That is mortality."

But that is *not* mortality. That is not what will be swallowed up or eaten up. As long as you are in the world, you will want the casket—and the body is the casket! But it is that which is in the body which is mortal. What is in the body will be eaten up with immortality.

If I would go through Romans, Galatians, Timothy, Luke, Mark, and Peter, I would find sixty-six different descriptions of mortality.

I would find sedition, heresy, envy, strife, malice, hatred, murder, emulation, witchcraft, covetousness, adultery, and fornication included among them. All these are mortality, but there is also a life in the supernatural which can eat them ALL up, devour them ALL, destroy them ALL, until there is no condemnation in this body at ALL.

The Scriptures are very clear: We must allow ourselves to come in touch with this great life in us, this wonderful life divine, this Christ-form, this spiritual revelation.

Do not forget, the Holy Ghost did not come as a cleanser. The Holy Ghost is NOT a cleanser; the Holy Ghost is *a revealer of imperfection,* which takes the blood of Jesus to cleanse. After the blood has cleansed the imperfection, you need the Word of God, for the Word of God is the only power which creates anew. Life comes through the Word. The Word is the Son. He that has received the Son has received life; he that has not received the Son has not life (1 John 5:12).

Millions of people living today don't have life, eternal life. Only one life is eternal life, and that is the life of the Son of God. One is a life of eternal death; the other, of eternal life. One is a life of destruction; the other, of eternal deliverance. One is a life of bondage; the other, of freedom. One is a life of sorrow; the other, of joy.

I want you to see that you are to live so full of the life divine that you are not moved by any wind of doctrine or *anything* which comes along.

People make the biggest mistake in the world and miss the greatest things of God today by turning to *the letter* instead of *the Spirit*.

How many people have spoiled their life because they "went mad" on water baptism? You cannot prove to me through any part of Scripture that baptism can save you, as they say. Baptism is only a form, yet people are mad, being firm that if you are not baptized, you are lost. These people get the letter, and the letter always kills. *The Spirit always gives life!*

The person, whoever he is, who would turn you from the baptism of Matthew 28 to any other baptism is a thief and a robber, and is trying to destroy you. Do not be carnally minded; be spiritually minded, for then you will know the truth, and the truth will make you free.

See to it that you know and affirm that it is Christ who gives life. Division in your thinking gives sorrow; it brings remorse, trials, and difficulties. Let Christ dwell in your hearts *richly*, by faith.

Don't go mad on preaching only on the baptism of the Holy Ghost. You will be lopsided!

Don't go mad on preaching water baptism. You will be lopsided!

Don't go mad on preaching healing. You will be lopsided!

There is only one thing that you will never go lopsided on, and that is the preaching of *salvation*. The only power is the Gospel of the kingdom. Men are not saved by baptism, not even by the baptism of the Holy Ghost, and especially not by the baptism in water. They are saved through the blood and preserved by the *blood*.

The Lord wants to bring us to the place of real foundation truth. Build upon the foundation truth. Don't be twisted aside by anything. Let this be your chief position: You are living to catch more of the Spirit—*only* the Spirit!

I clearly know that the baptism in the Holy Ghost is not the only thing that makes me eligible for the coming of the Lord. People have gone mad, thinking it is. They have gone mad because they have gotten baptized with the Spirit and think no one is right with God but those who are baptized with the Spirit. It is the biggest foolishness in the world. Why is it foolishness? Because the Truth bears it out. The thief on the cross went right up to meet Jesus in Paradise, and he was not baptized with the Spirit!

But just because a thief missed some good things, shall you miss them? No! It was the great grace of the Lord to have mercy upon him who didn't have them.

There is not a gift, not a grace, not a position that God will not give you to loosen you from your bodages. He wants you to be free in the Spirit. He wants to fill you with the Holy Ghost and the Word, until He brings you to the place of sealing of the Spirit.

The Sealing of the Spirit

You say, "What is the sealing of the Spirit?"

The sealing of the Spirit is when God has put His mark upon you and you are tagged .

Some people are troubled if they are "tagged" in the street when a man comes by them on horseback! But it is a wonderful thing to have the tag of almightiness. It seals you. The devil cannot touch you. It proves the Lord has preserved you for Himself. There is a covenant between you and God, and the sealing of the Spirit keeps you in that covenant, where evil powers have no more dominion.

Don't go away with the idea that I am preaching a perfection where you cannot sin. There is a place of perfection, of being purified as He is pure, so that we cannot commit sins. No man can commit sin if he is being purified. But it is when he ceases from seeking a deeper experience—a holier vocation, a deeper separation, a perfect place where he and Christ are one—that sin comes in.

Only in Christ is there security.

Let no man think that he cannot fall because he stands. No, don't think that. Remember this: You need not fall. Grace abounds where sin abounds; and where weakness is, grace comes in. Your very inactivity becomes divine activity.

Where absolute weakness is, so that you feel you cannot stand the trial, God comes in and enables you to stand. Life is ministered to you. Christ takes the place of weakness. You can say *"... when I am weak, then I am strong"* (2 Corinthians 12:10), for God touches you with His strength.

This is ideal. This is divine appointment. This is holy installation. This is God's thought from the throne. The Lord is speaking to us, and I would speak His words with a trumpet-voice to the whole world: "Be ye holy!"

Don't fail to see that God wants you ready for translation—holiness is the *habitation* of God.

Spiritual Drunkenness

There is a place to reach in the Holy Ghost which is mystifying to the world and to many people who are not going with God. It is remarkable: We can be so filled with the Spirit, so clothed upon, so purified within, so made ready for the Rapture, that we are drunk in the Spirit all the time!

> *For whether we be beside ourselves, it is to God: or whether we be sober; it is for your cause.*

2 Corinthians 5:13

Oh, to be so filled with the Spirit of life that you are absolutely drunken; completely beside yourself!

Now, when I come in contact with people who would criticize my drunkenness, I am sober. I can be sober one minute and drunk the next. But I tell you, to be drunk is wonderful! Ephesians 5:18 admonishes us, *"... be not drunk with wine, wherein is excess; but be filled* [drunk] *with the Spirit."*

A drunk man stops at a lamppost, and he has a lot to say to it. He talks the most foolish things possible. The people say, "He's gone."

Pray, *"O Lord, that I may be so drunk that it makes no difference what people think!"*

I am not concerned about what people think. I continue to speak to the Lord in hymns and spiritual songs, making my boast in the Lord. The Lord of hosts is 'round about me, and I am so free in the Holy Ghost that I am ready to "take off." But He does not take me.

Why doesn't He take me? I am ready to "take off" and it is better for me to go; but for the Church's sake, it is preferable to *stop*. It is preferable to be clothed upon, living in the midst of the people with no nakedness, full of purity, full of power, full of revelation, for the Church's sake.

Yes, it is far better to go; but for the Church's sake, to stop, that I may be helpful by telling the people how they can have their nakedness covered; how all their imperfections can be covered; how all the mind can be clothed; how all their inward impurities are made pure in the presence of God; and how to be living, walking, and acting in the Holy Ghost. This is wonderful, and this is the height God would have us to be at.

Here is a keynote verse to many positions we are holding in this subject of preparing for Rapture.

> *And if Christ be in you, the body is dead because of sin; but the Spirit is life because of righteousness.*
>
> Romans 8:10

There is no such thing as having liberty in your body if there is sin there. Only when righteousness is there, does righteousness abound. When Christ is in your heart, enthroning your life, and sin is dethroned, righteousness abounds, and the Holy Ghost has great liberty.

My, what triumphs of heights, of lengths, of depths, of breadths there are in the holy place! And where is the holy place? *Right inside us!* Right inside the children of God, the heirs of God, the joint-heirs with Christ!

Tongues Interpretation

> *He that is dead is free from sin, but alive unto God by the Spirit, and is made free from the law of sin and death. And he has entered into a relationship with God. Now God is his reward.*

He is not only a son but joined in heirship because of sonship. In purity, he is joined together with Him. And no good thing will He withhold from him, because he walks uprightly. Every good thing is for us on the holy line, walking uprightly, being set free, being made God's property.

Reconciliation in Christ

And all things are of God, who hath reconciled us to himself by Jesus Christ, and hath given to us the ministry of reconciliation;

To wit, that God was in Christ, reconciling the world unto himself, not imputing their trespasses unto them; and hath committed unto us the word of reconciliation.

2 Corinthians 5:18, 19

What is reconciliation? To be absolutely joined to Christ and blended with Him in atonement. Reconciliation is a glorious thing! We remember the blessed Son of God, taking our place in reconciliation, becoming the absolute position of all uncleanness, of every sin. God laid upon Him the iniquity of all, that every iniquity might go, every bondage might be made free. Sin, death, disease leaving; resurrection, re-creation entering!

When He comes, we shall not be naked, but clothed upon, separated, filled within, made like Him in every way.

I come to you only in the living fact of this testimony. To me, it is reality. I am living in it. I am moving in it. I am acting in it. And I am coming to you with the joy of it!

It is joy unspeakable and full of glory...
And the half has never yet been told.

I know that this life-divine, which is free from bondage, free from the power of Satan, free from evil thoughts, free from thoughts of evil, is for us. God is reconciling us in such a way to Himself that He abounds to us. In Him, we have:

FREEDOM!

PURITY!

POWER!

SEPARATENESS!

We are ready for the great trumpet!

(July 21, 1927)

About the Author

D R. ROBERTS LIARDON, author, public speaker, spiritual leader, church historian and humanitarian, was born in Tulsa, Oklahoma, the first male child born at Oral Roberts University. For this distinction he was named in honor of the university's founder. Thus, from the start of his life Roberts was destined to be one of the most well-known Christian authors and orators of the 20th century. To date he has sold over 7,000,000 books worldwide which have been translated in more then 50 languages and is known internationally, having ministered in over 112 countries.

An author of 54 books that continue to bless the body of Christ, Roberts continues to have a voice that speaks to this generation of believers and at the same time reaches out to those that are eager to read a relevant message that draws the heart closer to God.

Roberts' career in ministry began at a young age, when in 1979, he gave his first public address at the age of 13. Then at 17 he published his first book, *I Saw Heaven,* which catapulted him into the public eye. The book sold over 1.5 million copies and by the following year Roberts had become one of the leading public speakers in the Christian community all over the world.

God inspired Roberts shortly after the publication of *I Saw Heaven* to write and produce a book and video series entitled *God's Generals,* which chronicled the lives of some of our leading Pentecostal / Charismatic leaders. It was an immediate success and became one of the bestselling Christian video series in history and established Roberts as a leading Protestant church historian, a mantle he still wears to this day.

Roberts' notability increased outside Christendom as well. Twice he was voted as Outstanding Young Man in America. His popularity prompted international travel to be hosted by presidents, kings, leading political and religious leaders. Dignitaries the world over respect and admire the work and character of Roberts Liardon. His introductions include meeting with former President Ronald Reagan, former Prime Minister Lady Margaret Thatcher, and Dr. Billy Graham. Plus, he has received letters of commendation and honor from many others he has not met personally, including a letter from President George and Laura Bush honoring him for his commitment and contribution to improve the quality of life in his community.

In 1990 at the age of 25, Roberts Liardon moved to Southern California and established his worldwide headquarters in Orange County. Here he founded one of the largest Christian churches and Bible colleges in Orange County. Embassy Christian Center would become a base for his apostolic work that would include assistance to the poor and needy, not only in Southern California, but throughout the world. From his ministry he established, financed and sent forth close to 500 men and women to various nations on the globe. Over the years these humanitarian missionary teams have provided food, clothing, spiritual teachings, expertise and assistance to those in need.

Since the beginning of the millennium Roberts has continued to fulfill a demanding speaking schedule along with writing new books and mentoring a new generation of world leaders to effect change for the church and society. He continues to manage and expand his international headquarters in Sarasota, Florida and has an extension office in London, England.

OUR VISION

Proclaiming the truth and the power of the Gospel of Jesus Christ with excellence. Challenging Christians to live victoriously, grow spiritually, know God intimately.

Connect with us on

Facebook @ HarrisonHousePublishers
and Instagram @ HarrisonHousePublishing
so you can stay up to date with news
about our books and our authors.

Visit us at **www.harrisonhouse.com**
for a complete product listing as well as
monthly specials for wholesale distribution.